PSALMS FOR GOD'S PEOPLE
A Bible Commentary for Laymen

Robert K. Johnston

Regal Books

A Division of GL Publications
Ventura, California, U.S.A.

Rights for publishing this book in other languages are contracted by Gospel Literature International (GLINT) foundation. GLINT also provides technical help for the adaptation, translation, and publishing of Bible study resources and books in scores of languages worldwide. For further information, contact GLINT, Post Office Box 6688, Ventura, California 93006, U.S.A., or the publisher.

Third Printing, 1986

Published by Regal Books
A Division of GL Publications
Ventura, California 93006
Printed in U.S.A.

Library of Congress Cataloging in Publication Data

Johnston, Robert K., 1945-
   Psalms for God's people.

   Bibliography: p.
   1. Bible. O.T.   O.T. Psalms—Commentaries. I. Title
BS1430.3.J64   223'.207   82-5344
ISBN 0-8307-0820-0   AACR2

Contents

A Teacher's Manual and Student Discovery Guide for
Bible study groups using this book are available from
your church supplier.

Acknowledgments

The material for these chapters was first presented as part of a class on the Psalms which I was generously asked to teach at St. Mark's School of Theology, Auburn, Kentucky. The students were all men studying for the priesthood as their second vocation. These gentlemen sang the Psalms as part of their daily private and public worship. I learned much from them.

While on sabbatical, I have had the pleasure once again of teaching the Psalms at New College for Advanced Christian Studies in Berkeley, California. New College was founded in the late 1970s to provide graduate level Christian training for laypeople. If the students I had are any indication (a counselor, doctor, professor, homemaker, environmental engineer, InterVarsity staff member, nurse, real estate appraiser, and so on), the school has a bright future indeed. We need in our society a large body of well-informed Christians, able to integrate their evangelical faith and their vocations.

In order to test out my ideas, I asked my father and mother, Roy and Naomi Johnston, to teach a thirteen-week series on the Psalms in an adult Sunday School class at the Evangelical Covenant Church in Pasadena, California. I have benefited greatly from their suggestions and from the careful editing and typing of the manuscript which my mother provided. My parents have continued to instruct me in my response to our Lord. It is to them I dedicate this book.

Preface

In this guide into the book of Psalms, representative texts have been chosen, ones expressive of the variety of styles and themes found in the hymnbook of Israel's worshiping community. It is my hope that by studying these selected psalms, the relevance for today of the entire Psalter will become clearer. Here are the responses of believers to their God as they encountered a variety of life's experiences. Here should be found models for our responses as well.

The book of Psalms is, in Roland Murphy's words, a "school of prayer," in which we are both taught about the God we address and given models for presenting ourselves to Him. In the Psalms we learn about our God who is both transcendent and personal, majestic and caring. We also find examples of "the many motifs, aspirations, fears and hopes which can be employed by a community of faith."

The study of the Psalms cannot be merely an intellectual activity. These songs invite our meditation and personal interaction. If this book helps you to better appreciate the Psalms as your psalms, if it serves to encourage you to fill your minds and hearts with these inspired prayers of God's people to Him, then it will have served its purpose.

"Make a joyful noise to the Lord, all the lands! Serve the Lord with gladness! Come into his presence with singing!" (Ps. 100:1,2)

Robert K. Johnston

One

The Psalms: Songs for All God's People

(An Introduction)

The Old Testament is not a book of "secular" history; its concern is with "holy history." The Old Testament provides a record of God's saving words and deeds. Thus, events are chosen not with the "disinterestedness" of a historian but with the specific aim of showing who God is. God is a God who elects a people, covenants with them, rescues them in their time of need, reveals to them both His name and His desired pattern for life, brings them into the land He has chosen for them, and chastens and rewards them through judge and prophet.

The Old Testament's focus is on God and how He has spoken and acted—how He has revealed Himself to us. But it provides other perspectives as well, recording not only God's action, but Israel's reaction. It is in the Psalms in particular that we hear Israel's dialogue with God. It is here that we too are instructed in how to address our God.

The Judeo-Christian faith is a religion of relationship and response. God speaks so we can speak. God acts so we can act. The initiative is with God; the response from His people. The book of Psalms is God's inspired word just as surely as is the narration of the Exodus story. Its focus, however is not primarily on what God has done, but on what we can do. Its concern is not with what God has said, but with teaching us what we can say in return.

Understanding the Psalms

The title of the book of Psalms derives from the Greek translation (*psalmoi*) of the original Hebrew word *tehillim*, meaning "songs of praise." As we shall see in the chapters that follow, the Psalms contain other types of songs besides hymns of praise. But central to the collection of songs, whether they be characterized by thanksgiving or petition, by rejoicing or travail, is the realization that our God is a God worthy of praise.

As we seek to understand better the message and emotion of the psalms, three facts must be kept in mind: the psalms are (1) religious poems, (2) collected and arranged, (3) for use in worship.

The Psalms as religious poetry. While the book of Psalms is the main body of poetry in the Bible, its poetic style is not unique. Rather, it shares a long tradition and particular literary form with more than forty percent of the Old Testament. Many of the modern translations of the Old Testament take note of this fact by printing in poetic form such books as Nahum, Obadiah, Micah, and much of Isaiah. The fact that the psalms are poetry cannot be overstressed, for we read poetry—whether its language be Hebrew or English—with a different attitude and approach than we read prose.

In particular, there are two main characteristics

of biblical poetry that must be understood. The first is usually labeled *parallelism* and refers to the common practice of echoing the thought of one line in the next. As Roland Murphy observes, "Here is how the psalmist repeats without monotony." This repetition may take a variety of forms. The writer can, for example, restate in different words the exact thought which has been given in the previous line. This is called *synonymous parallelism* ("The Lord of hosts is with us; the God of Jacob is our refuge," Ps. 46:7; see also Ps. 1:5). Any nuance of difference between the synonyms (in our case, "the Lord of hosts" and "the God of Jacob," or "with us" and "our refuge") is incidental. The phrases are meant to reinforce each other, not compete.

Not all forms of Hebraic parallelism simply produce an echo. In *antithetic parallelism* the sense of the first line is taken up and repeated in the second by using its negative equivalent ("They will collapse and fall; but we shall rise and stand upright," Ps. 20:8; see also Ps. 1:6). Here again, just one idea is being offered, but it is expressed in both positive and negative terms.

A final poetic approach in the psalms is called *synthetic parallelism*. In this poetic form the second line takes up and expands on a thought begun in the first line ("The Lord is near to all who call upon him, to all who call upon him in truth," Ps. 145:18; see also Ps. 1:2). In our example, the second line helps clarify the first by stating a qualification concerning those who call on the Lord. It must be done "in truth." Sometimes this expansion can extend over several lines, the total unit forming a chain-like structure ("Ascribe to the Lord, O heavenly beings, ascribe to the Lord glory and strength. Ascribe to the Lord the glory of his name; worship the Lord in holy array," Ps. 29:1,2; see also Ps. 1:1). By spreading the point out over four lines, the poet is able to heighten the readers' interest and impress upon them the intended message.

Such is the basic structure of biblical poetry—parallelism. Neither rhyme nor rhythm is the chief characteristic, but the repetition of thought. (Contrast this with English poetry where rhyme and rhythm often are the pattern: "Roses are red, Violets are blue; Sugar is sweet, And so are you.") It is interesting to observe that because the poetic force of the psalms is based primarily on its parallelism of thought and not on its sound, little of its poetic impact is lost in translation. For this we can praise God.

The psalms as poetry portray truth not only in the form of repetition—taking the idea of one line and carrying it over into the next—but they often express these ideas by the use of *vivid images and symbols*. Here is a second major characteristic of the poetry of the psalms. Thus, in Psalm 65 we read, "The meadows clothe themselves with flocks, the valleys deck themselves with grain, they shout and sing together for joy" (Ps. 65:13). The listening reader hears not the language of philosophy or of science, but that related to aspects of everyday life. Truth is not argued or dissected; it is portrayed. In the psalms there is a passion, a singing from the heart, which expresses actual experience, not that which is merely imagined. But this is done through the use of a great variety of images and symbols. As T. S. Eliot once stated in discussing the task of poetry, it "is not the assertion that something is true, but the making that truth more fully real to us."

There are two particular aspects of the psalmists'

symbolic language which need special highlighting. The first is the tendency toward *hyperbole*, or exaggerated statement. In the psalms we hear the language of the heart. It is not always meant to be clinically analyzed and appropriated. For example, in Psalm 22 the writer prays for deliverance from serious danger or illness by pleading with God to be rescued from bulls (v. 12), from dogs (v. 16), and from lions (v. 21). The images are graphic and brutal and are meant to convey the fact that the psalmist feels forsaken by God (v. 1), little more than a worm (v. 6), and laid in the dust of death (v. 15). The passion and intensity of the psalmist need not be reduced in a literal manner to the multiple situations described. Rather, we must recognize that the writer is voicing his need graphically, intensely, and symbolically.

In this and other examples (see Ps. 69:1-3) we observe that the psalmists are not concerned with providing a detailed, precise "photograph" of the situation. Rather than objectively describe the exact state of affairs so that all can know the particular circumstances, the writers are content to *interpret their situations* in more *general terms*. Here is a second characteristic of the psalmists' use of symbolic language. The writers often retreat to anonymity, describing themselves and their situations in strong but conventional language. For example, although thirty or more of the psalms refer to "enemies" who hunt down, rob, spy, murder, insult and even await the psalmists' deaths, it has proved impossible to define more closely who these various evildoers are. The intention of the psalmists is not to hide their circumstances or to make their foes impersonal; rather, they are seeking to communicate the truth of their situation by universalizing it. Their poetic language is not meant to describe merely their own experience; it is also intended to be typical of all humanity.

The psalms' symbolism often frustrates those who would attach a specific date and circumstance to each song. But instead of reducing the psalms to objective historical situations, we would do better to let their poetry stir our hearts to share their praise and petition, which is timeless and appropriate to all of God's people everywhere. The psalms were written in particular circumstances; yet they are applicable to many. This is why they were used as Israel's hymnbook in worship and why Christians through the ages have made the words of the psalms their own. As Bernhard Anderson has said, "Because the Psalmist speaks as a poet he also speaks to us and for us."

The poetic form of the psalms, thus, is characterized by the uses of parallelism and symbolism. Together, these literary techniques increase the force and usefulness of the psalms to all peoples everywhere. By having a parallelism of thought, not word, little if any of the poetic force is lost in translation. Similarly, by using general, symbolic language, little of the meaning becomes dated or tied to a specific historical context. The psalms have a universal appeal. They are God's inspired songbook to be used by His people in all situations and times.

The Psalms as a collection. Psalms (songs) of God's people are not found only in the book of Psalms. They are found throughout the Bible, including the song of deliverance found in Exodus 15:1-18; the song of Moses, Deuteronomy 32; Deborah's victory song, Judges 5; the song of Hannah, 1 Samuel 2; David's song of deliverance, 2 Samuel 22, which is repeated in the Psalms as Psalm 18; King Hezekiah's song, Isaiah 38:9-20; Habakkuk's song, Habakkuk

3:2-19; and Jonah's prayer from the fish's belly, which was a song of thanksgiving, Jonah 2:1-9. The books of Job and Isaiah contain many hymns and laments (see Isa. 42:10-12; Job 5:8-16; Job 9:4-10; Job 10:1-22). Psalms of lament are found in Jeremiah and in the book of Lamentations.

These and many other examples reveal that the book of Psalms does not contain all of the hymns of Israel. No, Israel composed and sang songs for many occasions. The Psalms are not the exhaustive collection of all of Israel's worship songs. Rather, the book of Psalms is the inspired collection of Israel's songs which were used in her public worship—used to express her thanksgiving and her adoration, her petitions and her trust.

Most modern versions of the Bible follow ancient tradition in dividing the book of Psalms into five books (Pss. 1-41; 42-72; 73-89; 90-106; and 107-150). They do this because the Psalms turns out, on closer inspection, to be a collection of previous collections of songs, each with its own unique shape and characteristics. Each of the five collections, for example, ends with a doxology of praise which is not a specific ending to its final psalm, but a closing hymn of praise rounding out the whole collection (see Pss. 41:13; 72:18,19; 89:52; 106:48; and 150). One of these closing doxologies, the one concluding Book IV, is quoted by the Chronicler. Thus we see how it was used in worship (see Ps. 106:48 and 1 Chron. 16:35,36).

There are other indications that the book of Psalms was not written by one person at one given time but is rather a group of collections of songs that showed themselves to be divinely inspired. One of the strongest indications is the fact that several psalms appear twice in different "books" of the Psalms. For example, Psalms 14 and 53 are identical. (The psalm, it seems, was placed in two separate collections and not removed from either one when the collections were reverently brought together.) This is the case also with Psalm 70 and the second half of Psalm 40 (see vv. 13-17). It is also true of Psalm 108, which turns out to be a liturgy composed entirely from two other psalms (Ps. 57:7-11 and Ps. 60:5-12).

That the Psalms is a collection of collections is demonstrated also by the fact that many of the psalms are grouped into mini-collections according to content, author or title. The psalms of Book I (1-41) are largely attributed to David and are all individual psalms. Psalms 42 to 49 are assigned to the Sons of Korah and are for the most part community psalms; Psalms 51 to 72 again are Davidic; Psalms 73-83 are ascribed to Asaph, a musician who founded a Temple service guild; Psalms 93 to 99 are the enthronement psalms; Psalms 120 to 134 are labeled "Songs of Ascents," psalms perhaps sung during the Israelites' annual pilgrimage up to Jerusalem; Psalms 146 to 150 all begin with "Hallelujah" (that is, "Praise the Lord"). Like our contemporary hymnals, the book of Psalms grew from smaller collections.

Again, it is instructive to note that while Psalm 72 ends with the statement; "The prayers of David, the son of Jesse, are ended" (Ps. 72:20), more psalms of David appear later in the Psalter (see Pss. 108-110 and 138-145). The most probable explanation for this final verse of Psalm 72 is that it originally closed one of the collections of inspired worship songs that were later combined to form the book of Psalms. Moreover, this collection was associated chiefly with

David.

A final indication that the Psalms is made up of collections comes as we note that the terms used to address God tend to change from collection to collection. While Books I, IV, and V use the term "Lord" (Heb., *Yahweh*) almost exclusively, Book II and part of Book III (Ps. 42 to 83) prefer the term "God" (Heb., *Elohim*). Just as one generation of Christians uses the term "thou" in their worship, while another prefers the term "you," so the early Israelites in their worship seem to have shown preference for one or another term for God. Here, perhaps, is the reason that two of the psalms noted above appear in otherwise identical form: Psalm 14 makes use of the name "Lord," while Psalm 53 uses "God."

Throughout the Bible, David is identified with the psalms (see 2 Sam. 23:1; 1 Chron. 23:5; Amos 6:5; Heb. 4:7; Rom. 4:6-8; Acts 4:25,26). Nearly one-half of the Psalter (seventy-three psalms) has the superscription attached "of David." It is, however, significant that many psalms are attributed to others (twelve psalms to Asaph; eleven to the Sons of Korah; Psalm 90 to Moses; Psalm 88 to Heman; Psalms 72 and 127 to Solomon) and that thirty-four psalms remain anonymous. Moreover, while David no doubt wrote many of the psalms, it is useful to know that the term "of David" can also mean in Hebrew "by," "for," or "concerning" David.

David was Israel's favorite psalmist and his influence on Israel's hymnody, direct and indirect, was so strong that the entire book of Psalms came to be identified with him. Psalms is David's book. But we must recognize that others wrote psalms also and that some psalms even assigned to David might be intended "in honor of David" or "in the style of

David." We cannot be sure from the information given us in the Bible who the original author is of many of the psalms.

Our openness concerning the authorship of certain psalms (but *not* concerning the biblical witness that Israel's hymnody is rooted in and shaped by David) is also based on the fact that the psalms' individual titles (for example, Ps. 80: "To the Choirmaster: according to Lilies. A Testimony of Asaph. A Psalm") are not part of the original, inspired Scriptures. The titles are later comments upon the psalms (sometimes centuries after their origin). This is why in many translations, the titles and technical descriptions are not numbered in the verses. The titles come from a period later in Israel's history when devout Jews who had studied the psalms and investigated the traditions associated with them wrote down the historical and liturgical context which they thought should be associated with each particular psalm. Some psalms remained anonymous, but for others titles were provided to illumine the psalms and to aid the worshiper.

Just as we noted in our discussion of the Psalms as poetry, so we observe here a universal quality to the Psalms. While we moderns are uncomfortable with anonymity, the early Israelites were not. As historical details were helpful in revealing a psalm's meaning, they were sometimes remembered, passed on from generation to generation, and eventually recorded. But more typically, we find in the Psalms not songs of merely one person and place, but songs of God's people appropriate to all people and places. Even those songs assigned specifically to David often defy specific analysis as to the occasion for their composition. These psalms are David's God-inspired gift to us all, his response to his God and ours.

The Psalms intended for worship. It has been suggested that the Psalms are divided into five "books" in order to parallel the five books of the Law (Genesis, Exodus, Leviticus, Numbers, Deuteronomy). In their worship at the synagogue, furthermore, the Israelites divided the Pentateuch into just over 150 assigned readings. It is likely that the 150 psalms were used as companion texts to the reading of God's Law. If these surmises are true, we find evidence that the Psalms had a public or corporate character. They were sung by all of God's people in their worship in responding to their God.

The psalms of the Bible, though composed by individuals under the inspiration of God, are *not* merely expressions of individual thoughts and feelings. Rather, they are the songs of God's people. The psalms, even when voiced in the first person singular ("I," "me"), have about them a basic universality. "My" song is really "our" song; "my" prayer, "our" prayer.

In an era when life has been wrongly divided into the sacred and the secular it is hard for us to realize the importance of worship in Israel's life. Worship was widespread and related to the whole of life's experiences. Thus when you planted a field you had a religious ceremony. When you harvested your crop you did likewise. When you were sick you came to God for help along with God's people. When you sinned you sought in worship forgiveness and restitution. When your king was enthroned you first of all worshiped God. All of the psalms, even those originally composed concerning specific events (fourteen are linked, for example, to specific episodes in David's career), have a universality of tone and theme. They were used in the context of Israel's on-going worship.

They are the songs of God's people as they repeatedly responded to His presence (or absence) among them.

Until the turn of this century, Christians usually studied the psalms by searching out their historical background. But as a survey of the great nineteenth-century commentaries will indicate, there was little consensus in the scholars' findings. (Only those psalms specifically linked by their titles to episodes in David's life were treated in a standard way.) Although battles were mentioned in the psalms, it was impossible to know which specific battles. Although enemies were referred to time and again, rarely could they be identified with certainty. A "sanctified imagination" is fine in some situations, but used in the study of the Psalms, it proved inadequate.

Around 1900 a new approach to the study of the Psalms was explored. Rather than concentrate on the original historical setting of each psalm, students of the Bible turned to examine the Psalms' setting in Israel's worship. Given the central place of the Psalms in the Temple and synagogue, some began to ask of each psalm not, Why was it originally written? or, When? but, How was it used by God's people to direct their worship of God? Such a fresh approach to the Psalms did not invalidate the insights of other methods. But it soon became evident that it did allow the message of the Psalms to be exposed in a fresh way.

Indexing Israel's Worship Book

As faithful scholars addressed the Psalms as being God's uniquely-intended worship book for His people, they discovered that the Psalms contain several basic types or kinds of psalms, each suitable for a typical occasion for worship. Just as we can distinguish between prayers most suitable for a presiden-

tial inauguration or a community-wide ecumenical
Thanksgiving service or a Wednesday-night prayer
meeting, so we have been able to recognize certain
basic kinds or types of prayers in the Psalms. Just as
we can look in the index to find groupings of songs in
our modern hymnbooks (songs of praise, songs of
trust, songs about Jesus, songs for use in time of
need, Christmas carols), so we can index the psalms
according to their basic types of worship responses
(songs of individual and group petition, songs of
trust, hymns of praise, songs of thanksgiving, royal
psalms, wisdom psalms, and so on).

As such indexing was done, it was noted that
psalms suitable for given aspects of worship (praise,
thanks, petition, and so on) tend to follow a common
pattern of development and organization. The psalmists did not compose their songs of worship out of
thin air. Instead, inspired by God, they followed certain standard outlines or patterns expressing God's
intended message in the forms suitable to their worshiping community's expectation. Just as the leader
of worship in our churches accepts the standard procedures and orders of service of a given congregation
and expresses his or her unique message in light of
the expected form, so too did the psalmist. There are
exceptions in the Psalms where no typical pattern is
discernible. But what students of the Psalms widely
recognize is that the exceptions are just that—exceptions. More typical is the presence of certain general
forms that have helped to shape the Psalms.

That the Psalms reflect standard patterns of worship may come as a surprise to some. But we should
not forget that God's revelation has always come in
ways suitable for and understandable to us. This is
the wonder and glory of the Incarnation itself, when

God even became a man so that we could know Him. Throughout the Bible we observe God using the ideas, thought forms, and expectations of His inspired authors in their particular setting to communicate His Word to us. The Bible is "God's-Word-as-human-words." This is true of the Psalms as well.

In the chapters which follow we shall study representative psalms, those typical of the major forms of worship in Israel's life. We will seek to let God instruct us in our own worship by learning how Israel responded to her God. Psalms will be chosen not only for their uniqueness but because they typify a larger *group* of psalms. Many of the psalms' groupings reflect a similar outline and common style, and this will be noted. (For example, the Israelites expressed their thanksgiving to God in standard ways.) In other chapters the grouping will be based on a common situation or theme. (The psalms relating to Israel's king are one example; they share a thematic unity.) Basic to our approach to the psalms is the recognition that they can be divided into groups having more or less typical forms (outlines), themes, and worship settings.

The Psalms and the New Testament

The *final* section of many of the chapters will relate a given psalm to the teachings of the New Testament. This is for two reasons: First, because God's unfolding revelation is consistent and unified. What we later learn in the New Testament of God's relationship with His people and His people's relationship with Him fits the witness that the psalms have already provided. Along with the book of Isaiah, the Psalms is more frequently quoted than any other Old Testament book. It is therefore useful, in arriving at a fuller understanding of the message of the Psalms, to inquire into its New Testament application and extension.

Second, the relationship of the Psalms to the New Testament is taken up at the end of our discussion of a given book, and not at the beginning, for we want to focus our study in the psalms themselves. It is too easy in our study of the Old Testament to leap quickly into the New. The result is that we lose something of the rich perspective that the Old Testament has to teach us. Jesus considered the Psalms fully authoritative as Scripture and so should we. Our primary goal in this study will be to grasp the Israelites' understanding of the Psalms. What was the original intention of these songs to God? What can we learn from them concerning our worship of God?

One of the glories of Scripture is its built-in system of checks and balances. If we are prone to misread Paul's stress on "justification by grace alone," we have James's admonition that "faith without works is dead." If we would judge others responsible for their suffering because of our misreading of the book of Proverbs, we are corrected by Job. Each book of the Bible has its own authority and its own perspective. Yet all the books are but one book, God's Book for us. It is this fundamental concern to let each part of Scripture be heard on its own terms while not overlooking the Bible's overarching unity that has governed the writing of this book. The psalms must be listened to in their own context. Their profound understanding of faith, their uniquely expressed responses to their God, their familiarity with and fear of the Lord need to become the experience of Christians everywhere.

Discussion Questions

1. As an exercise in working with the poetry of the psalms, try to find synonymous, synthetic, and antithetic parallelisms in Psalm 1, as well as the use of symbolic language.

2. How does Psalm 1 serve as an introduction to the five books of the Psalms?

3. How are the titles of the psalms to be understood?

4. In what ways do the psalms have a universal appeal to their readers?

5. The psalms are God's-Word-as-human-words. What difference does it make in our study of them that they are God's Word? That they are human words?

Two

Psalm 13: From Grief to Joy

(An Individual Lament)

Should you complain to God in public? Before you answer the question, it will perhaps be useful to recall Jesus' words on the cross, "My God, my God, why hast thou forsaken me?" (Mark 15:34). These words of complaint were not original with Jesus but were quoted from Psalm 22:1. It is important to note also that such a complaint is not exceptional in the Psalms, this being only one of forty or more.

How was it that the Israelites complained publicly in prayer to their God so freely, so impiously (seemingly)? Shouldn't they have been more respectful and polite in God's presence? Shouldn't they have put their best foot forward and expressed only positive thoughts? Walter Brueggemann observes, "A study of the lament may be a corrective for some religion in the church which wishes to withdraw from life as it really is, to pretense and romance in the unreal world of heavenly or holy things. The lament [those psalms of complaint] makes clear that faith and worship deal with and are shaped by life as it comes to us."

Israel understood that life includes both bad and good, loneliness as well as fellowship, disease along with health, anxiety as well as peace, sorrow intermingled with joy. The life of the believer is not all sweetness and light; it never has been, as Psalm 13 attests. Life need not be represented to God in rosy hues that do not exist. We need not be Pollyannas; we need not praise God superficially for adversity. The psalm writers are able in the end to praise their Lord, but only after moving from grief to joy. Along the way they express real agony. We need not whitewash evil and suffering. It is when faith is recognized as being in crisis that it can be reaffirmed and strengthened. It is then that real joy can be experienced.

Psalm 13: An Individual Lament

There is in Psalm 13 a basic reversal in attitude: from complaint to trust, from desolation to delight, from grief to joy, from distress to rest. This change of perspective characterizes not only Psalm 13, but almost one-third of all the psalms. (See Pss. 3; 5; 6; 7; 13; 17; 22; 25; 26-28; 31; 35; 36; 38-40; 42; 43; 51; 54-57; 59; 61; 64; 69-71; 86; 88; 102; 108; 109; 130; 139-143.) Such psalms are usually called Psalms of Individual Lament. As these psalms accomplish such a radical transformation in mode, they follow a typical pattern: (1) the address; (2) the complaint; (3) the petition; (4) the motivation; (5) the assurance of being heard; and (6) a vow of offering.

We can best understand Psalm 13 by considering it in terms of these elements, or constitutive parts.

The address (v. 1a). It is important to realize that the psalmist's lament is addressed to someone. "O Lord," he cries (see also Pss. 4:1; 5:1). Israel, even in her hurt, recognizes her ongoing relationship with her God. It is only in the presence of God that her deepest hurts can be dealt with. The psalmist calls God by name: "Yahweh (O Lord), answer me."

The psalmist doesn't embellish his address with flattery. It is enough to reaffirm the covenantal context between God and His people when God revealed to Moses that His name was *Yahweh*, meaning "I am the one who is present to you and available" (see Exod. 3:13-15). God said that He was the psalmist's God; now the psalmist responds, accepting that fact as his starting point. He does not shy away from direct address; neither does he address God as a stranger. He comes to Him in faith, as is appropriate for a child of God.

Too often we talk to everyone except the principal party involved with our problem. We don't go to our employer with our complaint, but to our fellow worker. We express only positive sentiments and politeness to our superiors. We don't confide in our spouse about our feeling of sexual inadequacy, but rather speak about it to our best friend. We shy away from looking directly at the person we are correcting. In contrast to this general pattern of American culture, the ancient Israelite recognized that God alone was in charge and must be addressed. Israel expected change and honestly expressed herself to the God who could change things. The psalmist has no illusion that he will pull himself up by his own bootstraps. Nor is there a turning inward to find peace in meditation or positive thinking. Rather, the psalmist brings his predicament to God.

Dietrich Bonhoeffer, in his brief meditation on the Psalms, states: "There is in the Psalms no quick and easy resignation to suffering. There is always struggle, anxiety, doubt. . . . But even in the deepest hopelessness God alone remains the one addressed." It is significant that these comments were first published in 1940 in the midst of Bonhoeffer's church's persecution by Hitler. They were also written in the general context of Bonhoeffer's decision to remain in Germany and be with his people in their time of anguish and suffering, even if it meant his imprisonment and murder by Hitler, which it did. Bonhoeffer had learned his lesson well from the Psalms and his life of prayer remained constant throughout his ordeal. He observed that "serious illness and severe loneliness before God and men, threats, persecution, imprisonment, and whatever conceivable peril there is on earth are known by the Psalms." Moreover, they are not only *known*; they are expressed to God. "God alone remains the one addressed. Neither is help expected from men. . . . [The psalmist] sets out to do battle against God for God."

The complaint (lament; vv. 1,2). The central body of a typical Psalm of Lament consists of the complaint and the petition, either of which can come first and both of which are oft repeated. In Psalm 13 the complaint comes first as the psalmist pours out his distress: "How long, O Lord? Wilt thou forget me for ever?"

It is typical of this lament, as well as of others, that the language of the complaint is so generalized that the exact nature of the psalmist's suffering is now uncertain. The sense of danger before enemies is rarely clarified—Psalms 17:9; 35:4; the source of shame is not delineated—Psalms 4:2; 22:6; the sense of loneliness seldom explained—Psalms 31:11; 38:11. Why is the writer languishing in Psalm 6:2? Why is he "groaning" in Psalm 102:5? We can't be sure. So too with Psalm 13.

Was it persecution by an enemy that caused the writer's general dislocation? And what kind of enemy? Was it an act of God? Was it illness, as might be implied from verse 3? Perhaps illness was one result of outside pressures or of spiritual torment. We cannot say. What we can say is that the interconnectedness of life is demonstrated here, as it is also in our lives.

As anyone who is involved in it knows full well, suffering has to do with the whole of experience. One's relationships in the world affect one's attitude toward oneself and one's relationship with God, and vice versa. It is inconceivable to the psalmist, both here and in the other laments, that one's individual existence would lack a social dimension (in this case, his enemies) and a theological dimension (God). Even today it is recognized that theology, psychology, and sociology are all interrelated. Psalm 13 witnesses to this fact.

The psalmist finds himself involved in a *destructive circle* of relationships in which suffering in one area causes suffering in others. What is needed is *decisive* intervention from outside—a breaking of the circle. It is this that motivates the psalmist to seek God's help.

Notice the increased force of the complaint as it is put into poetic form. The psalmist repeats his cry four times: "How long?" Certainly the thrust of his lament is communicated with his first utterance, but the full force of his distress comes only through his repeated cries of anguish which spell out his despair in terms of the psalmist's relationship to God ("wilt thou hide"), to himself ("must I bear pain"), and to his enemy ("shall my enemy be exalted").

The psalmist uses carefully chosen language to

express his distress. His words are used for their
symbolism and force. They are also part of the poetry.
The language is the language of exaggeration. It is
not meant to be a scientific description of the psalmist's predicament, but is selected to convey the situation as he experienced and felt it. Two examples will
serve to illustrate this. In verse 1, "forget" and "hide
thy face" both have to do with the seeming absence of
God's practical help in this time of distress and with
God's perceived remoteness. The writer longs for intimate fellowship with his God (see also Pss. 11:7;
17:15).

A final observation on verses 1 and 2 will assist
the reader of Psalm 13. The *RSV*, in its translation of
verse 2, has adopted the Syriac variant "pain" instead
of the difficult Hebraic term meaning "counsel." But
"counsel" seems preferable. Given God's "absence,"
the psalmist has had to hold counsel with himself, a
fact which has caused him inner turmoil and sorrow.

The petition and its motivation (vv. 3,4). "Consider and answer me, O Lord my God; lighten my
eyes" (v. 3). The psalmist wants relief. He has not
raised his complaints solely for the therapeutic value
of complaining. He has come to God seeking an
answer. "Consider my situation, Lord, and lighten
my burden. Act, lest I die and my enemies prevail!"

In this psalm as in others, the psalmist includes
in his lament specific reasons why God should act at
this particular time. The intensity of his plea is seen
as the psalmist rallies all the support he can to help
convince his God to intervene now. He realizes that
he must touch Yahweh's heart. He must attempt to
move Yahweh to act. In other Psalms of Lament,
appeal is sometimes made to God's reputation (see
the discussion of Psalm 137 in chapter 5). At other

times, God's past action is cited as a reason for His present intervention—Psalms 22:4,5; 143:5. Often the psalmist protests his/her innocence—Psalms 26:4-7; 35:7, and helplessness—Psalms 25:16; 55:18. Many of the psalms attempt to persuade God by declaring the psalmist's basic and continuing trust in God—Psalms 56:3,4; 146:6. In Psalm 13 the psalmist bases his petition on two arguments. He cries out to God for help (a) lest he die (v. 3), and (b) lest his enemies rejoice over his calamity (v. 4).

Although the psalmist attempts to influence God's judgment and subsequent action, there is no romanticized notion that he is somehow an equal participant in the struggle. There is, rather, the full recognition that the psalmist's destiny is in Yahweh's hands. There is nothing more the author can do. If salvation (*salus*, health) is to come, it will be an act of pure grace. There is no possible cooperation implied. The psalmist is helpless; only Yahweh can transform this situation.

The statement of assurance and vow of offering (vv. 5,6). "My heart shall rejoice in thy salvation. I will sing to the Lord" (vv. 5,6). Having uttered his complaint and voiced his petition, the psalmist switches gears abruptly and openly declares that a change has indeed been effected. Just as the psalm begins with a forthright address to the Lord, even amidst the anguish, so it ends confidently in grateful trust in Him. The writer of Psalm 13 expresses his confidence by rejoicing in Yahweh's salvation (v. 5) and by pledging to sing to Yahweh for "he has dealt bountifully" with him (v. 6). His statements are so forceful that the reader might think the request had already been granted. (See also Pss. 26:12; 54:7.) It had!

What has allowed this change of heart? How has the psalmist recovered his equilibrium so quickly? No doubt it is tempting for some to question whether the suffering was real or merely feigned. But nowhere does our text (or other numerous laments) allow for such a watering down of the transformation. The impending defeat was real, not imagined; and so too the victory. How did this happen? The psalm writer does not answer our question directly, but let us look at two directions toward which our text seems to point:

First, a transformation takes place as the name of the Lord is spoken. In prayer, the psalmist is delivered from his travail. Peter expresses this same pattern of going from anxiety to rest as he admonishes: "Humble yourselves therefore under the mighty hand of God, that in due time he may exalt you. Cast all your anxieties on him, for he cares about you . . . [know] that the same experience of suffering is required of your brotherhood throughout the world. And after you have suffered a little while, the God of all grace, who has called you to his eternal glory in Christ, will himself restore, establish and strengthen you" (1 Pet. 5:6-10).

John provides another New Testament parallel. He quotes Jesus: "Whatever you ask in my name, I will do it, that the Father may be glorified in the Son; if you ask anything in my name, I will do it" (John 14:13,14). John declares the power of prayer in the name of the Lord. Centuries earlier the psalmist had illustrated it.

Second, the movement from anguished petition to joyful praise is decisive. And the psalmist's bold confidence before the Lord, his forthright prayer to his all-powerful and gracious Lord was no doubt instrumental in the process. Important as well was the example and support of his worshiping community. Some scholars believe that many of the Psalms of Lament were uttered in the Temple in the presence of the priest, who then spoke God's word of healing (salvation). This cannot be proven decisively, although it seems likely in the case of many of the laments. (See 1 Kings 8:37-40; Ps. 12:5.) It was as they worshiped that the Israelites found their confidence restored.

Conclusion

The psalmist is able to express his grief and anguish in a set worship form that is typical of the response of other believers. As we have seen, this form includes elements of address, complaint, petition, motivation, assurance, and vow. The psalmist, in other words, finds within his community of faith a general pattern of expression that helps direct his cry, a pattern which emphasizes the need for direct address to God, for honesty in one's expression of need and frustration, and for trust that God is in command of every situation. The psalmist is not alone as he attempts to deal with his crisis, nor is he the only one to experience crisis. He can thus learn from other believers how to move from grief to joy, and he does.

We cannot definitely answer the question of how a change of mood and situation was accomplished. God works individually in our hearts and lives. But that the psalmist's life is restored and that his health is renewed and his enemies overcome is boldly asserted. Important in this transformation process are both the honest, direct approach to God which is taken and the typical pattern of prayerful complaint (which includes statements of trust) which is adopted. Here are clues for us too. In our crises we need to address God personally. We also need to use such resources in the community of faith as this psalm to teach us how best to pray.

As individuals and as a church we have too often been intimidated by suffering and failure. "The victorious Christian life" has been wielded as a club to silence us. The Psalms of Individual Lament can teach us a central means of dealing with life's misery and agony. How can the faithful today cope with life's extremities, with those question marks that defy rational analysis? The Israelites learned to express their agony in the form of a prayerful public complaint or lament, a form that brought their questioning into the realm of faith and the community of faith, where they also shared renewed trust.

Discussion Questions

1. Is it possible to think of humankind in purely psychological terms? or sociological? or theological? Or are these three dimensions of one's total being, indissolubly connected (see Rom. 1:18-32)?

2. What rescues the laments of the psalmist from degenerating into expressions of self-pity?

3. How are Psalm 13 and the hymn "Sweet Hour of Prayer" similar? different? What reasons can you give for the differences?

4. Some of us are willing to express our complaints privately to God, but are we willing to state them also in the context of our public worship? Are we given the opportunity? Would such statements be helpful either to us or to the Christian community at worship?

5. Psalm 22, a Psalm of Individual Lament similar to Psalm 13, is spoken by Jesus in the passion account. What does this suggest about Jesus? What consolation does this offer us?

Three

Psalm 51: Confession, a Lost Art?

(A Penitential Psalm)

There was a movement within the evangelical church several years ago to do away with the act of confession. Instead, Christians were to turn any consciousness of sin they might have into expressions of trust and thanksgiving for the fact that on the cross these had once and for all been forgiven. It was argued that for those who believe in Jesus as Lord and Saviour, their sins—past, present, and future—had been buried, and they were reckoned (judged) righteous by God. Thus, the argument went, to confess was to demonstrate a lack of faith in what God had already done. Instead of confessing we should rejoice in the fact of our present imputed righteousness.

Those who in this manner questioned the need for confession were not denying that Christians continue to sin. Instead, they were reacting to the self-flagellation and neurotic guilt that seemed to characterize some Christians. Where was the joy of the victorious Christian living? they asked. Wanting to be submissive to Scripture, such Christians had trouble with 1 John 1:1-10, which calls us to confession. But in interpreting its call to confession as a single action in the past, an action with ongoing consequences, these Christians believed themselves to be biblical. If we *have* confessed our sins then they are forgiven. If we walk in the light we are already cleansed. All that is needed is for us to rejoice in our salvation. Such was the reinterpretation.

Now this interpretation of Scripture, although well-intentioned and perhaps even useful for those unable to move beyond their guilt, is not consistent with the biblical message. First John declares that we deceive ourselves if we say we are sinless. Moreover, we are told to confess our sins so we can be forgiven and our relationship with God restored. Psalm 51 is a second important witness. When we *transgress* God's law, it is important to confess our sin and cry out for mercy. Verbal confession is not the only context in which believers can approach God, but surely it is one necessary and significant way.

Before investigating the confessional perspective of Psalm 51, it is helpful to compare the psalm generally with others found in the Psalter. As we do this, we observe that its posture of confession is exceptional in the Psalter. The Christian church has for centuries made the seven Penitential Psalms (Pss. 6; 32; 38; 51; 102; 130; 143) which are found in Israel's songbook their favorites. These humble confessions have been singled out for special status; in the monasteries, for example, they were sung or prayed several times a day. In the process, confession has been made *the rule* in our worship. (Such New Testament teachings as the Lord's Prayer have reinforced this concern.) But in the Psalms, the explicit recognition of sin and guilt is more *the exception.* In fact, only these seven psalms out of the 150 included in Israel's book of worship (the Psalms) mention the author's sin. What does this mean for us today as we attempt as Christians to learn from this psalm and others how to respond to our God? Must we "correct" this lack of emphasis on confession which is found in the Psalter? Three responses can be given:

First, although petition for forgiveness of sins is rare in the Psalms, an awareness of sin is deeply rooted in many of the other psalms. For the psalmists, their happiness and well-being were linked directly to the state of their present relationship with God. (See chap. 12.) God was a God who rewarded righteousness and punished sin. Thus, to ask God to intervene in a time of distress was to ask indirectly for forgiveness at the same time. A special plea for forgiveness of sins was not considered necessary. It is implicit in the cry for help.

Secondly, although an awareness of sin is more prevalent in the book of Psalms than the few direct references to it might indicate, it is nonetheless a fact that explicit confession is not always included in the psalmists' responses to God. In fact, just the opposite is the case at times. In speaking with God, some of the psalmists have the boldness to declare their personal innocence and righteousness ("My steps have held fast to thy paths, my feet have not slipped" Ps. 17:5; see also 18:20-24; 26:1-12; 41:12; 59:3,4). It is not that the psalm writers would deny any sin if they were quizzed about it. Rather, in their current dialogue with God, confession is not the point. Thus personal innocence is asserted. Something else has captured their attention, and so they focus upon that (for example, petition or thanksgiving).

From these counterexamples where confession is explicitly excluded, we can perhaps learn to put confession in a more biblical perspective. Confession is central in our salvation and to our ongoing walk with the Lord. Moreover, it is appropriate and indeed is commanded that we voice our wrongdoing as we become conscious of our sin. But confession is not the only or even the major posture that God's children should have before Him. Praise, adoration, petition, thanksgiving—these are the responses to our merciful God that more commonly recur in the Psalter.

Thirdly, though confession need not dominate our ongoing walk with the Lord nor always intrude in our conversations with Him, neither can it be ignored. As it is needed, so it must be voiced, with passion and resolve. Too often our confession becomes little more than a "throw-away line," an expected litany repeated by rote. It is rarely heartfelt, particularly when it is included in our public worship services. We need help in recovering the ability to confess. And here Psalm 51 provides one important model. Rather than blandly and repetitively confess our sin, even when we can't pinpoint any sins, this psalm indicates that our confession should be more direct and heartfelt. "Say what you mean, and mean what you say!" Such is the perspective of Psalm 51 concerning the confession of sin.

Psalm 51: A Psalm of Lament

As we have observed in chapter 2, the almost fifty Psalms of Individual Lament have a general shape or pattern in common. Typically: (1) These psalms begin with a direct *address* to God, often with an introductory call for help; (2) then there follows a *lament*, expressing the anguish of the psalmist over his situation, as well as his relationships with both God and his enemies; (3) a *petition* is made and (4) additional supporting *reasons* are offered; finally, (5) the psalmist finds his grief removed and (6) declares his *assurance* that God has heard and responded to him; therefore he *vows* to praise God in His sanctuary.

It is helpful to remind ourselves of this general pattern for a Psalm of Lament in order to appreciate both the similarities and the differences between Psalm 51 and other laments. For Psalm 51 contains, like other laments, an invocation and introductory call for help (vv. 1,2), a petition (vv. 6-12), and a vow to praise God for His salvation, along with a statement of trust in the Lord (vv. 13-17). But what has been significantly recast is the lament (vv. 3-5). We note as well the addition of a final refrain (vv. 18,19), calling on God to intervene on behalf of all His people so that their worship will be acceptable in God's sight. We will need to inquire why the psalmist includes this.

The address: confessing to God (vv.1,2). The psalmist begins his song directly and passionately. He knows exactly what he needs (forgiveness) and therefore speaks to his God accordingly. Who is his God? The God of steadfast love. (The Hebrew word *hesed*, steadfast love, is one of the richest in the Old Testament and defies translation. God's *hesed* is His "loving-kindness," His "mercy," His "goodwill" and "beneficence." It is His "grace" and His "bounty.") The psalmist cries out in his need, asking God in His mercy to cleanse him. The radically personal nature of this psalm's address can be observed as its invocation is compared with one from an ancient Babylonian lament. There the penitent prays:

> O God whom I know or do not know,
> my transgressions are many;
> great are my sins;
> O Goddess whom I know or do not know,
> my transgressions are many;
> great are my sins . . .
> How long, O my Goddess whom I know
> or do not know,
> ere thy hostile heart will be quieted?

The Babylonian lament is to an unknown god and goddess; Psalm 51 is to a God who has revealed Himself and His will to His people.

In declaring to his God that he is a sinner in need of grace, the psalmist emphasizes his situation by the use of three complementary expressions for his sin. The author is not suggesting that he has committed three different kinds of sin. To suppose this is to fail to understand the nature of Hebraic poetry (see chap. 1). Rather, the psalmist unfolds to his reader the full seriousness of his broken relationship with God by using different images for his sin. He has "sinned" (*ḥāttā'ti*) in the sense that he has missed the mark, made a mistake. (Prov. 19:2 uses this same word of someone who is so hasty with his feet that he misses his way.)

Again, the psalmist has committed "iniquity" (*awon*). The original meaning of this Hebrew word is still debated; it could mean either perverseness or going astray. But in either case the action is deliberate. As N. H. Snaith suggests, "It is not a question of slipping, but of deliberately going in for a long slide." "Iniquity" is, thus, more serious than "sin."

Lastly, the psalmist confesses his "transgression"

(*peshā*). The Hebrew word means *rebellion*. More-over, the rebellion is not a mere turning away from a standard or law, but active revolt against a person—against God. Here the full seriousness of the psalm-ist's sin is admitted. As he states in verse 4, it is against God and God only that he has sinned. Although others have been wronged, although the ramifications of his sin may be far-reaching, it is chiefly God who has been offended. Thus, it is to God that the psalmist confesses.

The lament: confessing sin's bondage (vv. 3-5). The nature of the introductory call for mercy and the succeeding cry for forgiveness cause the psalmist to depart from the typical pattern of a lament. For although his is a lament, it is not a complaint. God is absolutely justified in His sentence. Thus from his cry for cleansing, the psalmist turns not to decry his external situation but to confess his inner complic-ity. The focus of the lament is narrowed from its typi-cal concern with the psalmist's situation, the ene-my's action, and God's absence to a concentration upon the psalmist's sinful condition. It is this alone he laments.

Recognizing his sinful heart, the writer suffers both from being in bondage to himself and from being alienated from his God. "My sin is ever before me," he bemoans (v. 3). The psalmist's guilty con-science has immobilized him. Even when he looks backward to his childhood, he cannot find a time of innocence when he was free from guilt (v. 5). All the joy and gladness have departed from him (v. 8). He is a person preoccupied with himself, as the repeated personal references suggest ("my transgressions"; "my iniquity"; "my sin"; "have I sinned, and done . . . evil"; "I was brought forth in iniquity"; "in sin . . .

conceive[d]"). His requests for cleansing (v. 7) and for re-creation (v. 10) are not incidental to his concern. They are absolutely necessary. He cannot of himself escape guilt's bondage.

Coupled with his sense of self-alienation and self-preoccupation is the psalmist's awareness that his sin has broken off his relationship with God (v. 4). He does not question God's judgment; it is appropriate, given his offense. But the sense of God's righteousness, when coupled with the awareness of his unrighteousness, only increases his feeling of hopelessness. Shut off from God he is shut up with himself and his sin. It is this that the psalmist laments.

The petition: asking for restoration (vv. 6-12). The psalmist's cry to his God carries with it not only the burden of judgment for sin, it also suggests the possibility of salvation. If God will but act, the psalmist will be whiter than snow. If God will but act, he will be filled with joy and gladness. Recognizing that God is not only righteous but merciful, the psalmist pleads with God for restoration. If God will, He can blot out the sinner's iniquities and restore the joy of his salvation. Thus, the psalmist pleads with his God to forgive him.

The cry of Psalm 51 for forgiveness is a series of petitions that give one of the most comprehensive descriptions of God's gracious activity toward us which is found in Scripture: "teach me wisdom . . . purge me . . . wash me . . . fill me with joy and gladness . . . let the bones which thou has broken rejoice . . . hide thy face . . . blot out all my iniquities. Create . . . a clean heart . . . put a new and right spirit within me. Cast me not away . . . take not thy holy Spirit . . . restore . . . uphold. . . ." God's redeeming work has many dimensions.

Many of the psalmist's requests contain allusions to Israel's history with her God. In particular, the phrase "purge me with hyssop" recalls the ritual prescribed in the Law (Lev. 14) for allowing a healed leper to return to the community. The psalmist's sin has caused him to feel like a leper, an outcast, shameful and alone. There was nothing he desired more than to be restored to the fellowship of God and His people. Similarly, the psalmist's plea to God to "create" in him a clean heart harkens back to the language of Genesis 1 where God made the heavens and earth out of nothing. Nothing short of a comparable miracle would suffice for the psalmist. He must be re-created (or to use Jesus' words, "born again"). A third reference to Israel's past is found in the prayer to God to not take His Spirit from the psalmist. Removal of God's presence was synonymous with doom, as the record of Saul's dynasty illustrates vividly (1 Sam. 16:14).

The vow to praise and affirmation of faith (vv. 13-17). The recognition that God can blot out sin and create life anew causes the psalmist to declare to God that he will tell others of God's grace in effecting his salvation. His restoration will not only grant his petition, it will be a powerful witness to others as the psalmist shares the wonderful news of God's grace. Moreover, the psalmist finds himself confident that God will indeed act. From the depths of his opening cry for help, the psalmist has moved in his prayer to the confident assertion that God will not reject those who truly seek Him (v. 17). There is a note of triumph here. Though the psalmist has sinned, God will forgive and restore.

Psalm 51 is usually read as a Psalm of Personal Confession. And so it is. But it is not only a confes-

sion of the psalmist's sin, it is equally a confession of
God's righteousness. The psalmist is not making his
plea to an indifferent judge but to the "God of [his]
salvation" (v. 14). The psalmist vows, Deliver me and
I "will sing aloud of thy deliverance" (literally, "righteousness"; in the Hebrew, *sedaqah*). God's righteousness as judge is demonstrated in the fact that
He will save, that He will deliver. (It is interesting that
in modern Hebrew a *sedaqah* is a charitable gift.)

Psalm 51 is, however, even more than a confession of both a person's obsessive guilt and God's righteous love. It is also the confession of a resolve to help
others who are in similar situations. The stark reality
of unconfessed sin is that it estranges one from others and from God. The sinner becomes totally
wrapped up in himself or herself. He/she is unable to
speak authentically to others (see v. 15). The consequence of experiencing God's forgiveness, on the
other hand, is a freedom to again be a person-for-oth-
ers. The psalmist asks God to deliver him from the
shackles of guilt so that his tongue can "sing aloud of
thy deliverance" (v. 14) and so that he can "teach
transgressors thy ways" (v. 13). The psalmist recognizes the compelling nature of God's grace. He vows
to speak as one sinner to the next the good news of
God's salvation.

It is worth reflecting on this movement within the
psalm from self to God to others, for it reflects a surprising truth about God's grace. It is often repentant
sinners and not "saints" who are used by God to further His kingdom. There is serendipity, surely, in the
fact that God can take a person's sinful past and use
it as the occasion for proclamation to others of God's
grace. The psalmist sinned greatly. Yet his very mis-
deed was the occasion for the writing of Psalm 51, a

psalm that has taught God's ways to thousands.

The final refrain (vv. 18,19). The psalm is in one sense complete with verse 17. Certainly its structure as an Individual Lament is completed with its statement of assurance that God will accept as a sacrifice "a broken spirit." But it was recognized that the psalm's emphasis upon one's inner motives and attitude before God could be misinterpreted by others singing this hymn in the context of their ongoing worship. For the psalm writer was not trying to undercut the sacrificial system of his day. He was, rather, trying to speak to those situations not covered by sin or guilt offerings (see Lev. 4-6), those situations of serious intentional sin which the sacrificial system ignored. Furthermore, the psalmist was trying to ground all worship in one's love and devotion to his or her God. For these reasons, the psalm makes in conclusion one final plea to God. It asks God to "do good to Zion," that is, to accept her broken spirit and restore her to prosperity. Then her worship would be sheer delight, her offerings pleasing and acceptable in God's sight. What the psalmist has asked for himself, the psalm now asks also for all of God's people. There is no selfishness or self-centeredness here. The psalm's desire is for all God's people to experience the joy of fellowship with God which the psalmist has known.

Conclusion

Psalm 51 is intended to instruct the whole of God's people. For as Paul later wrote, "All have sinned and fall short of the glory of God" (Rom. 3:23). For some, unfortunately, confession has been reduced, whether consciously or unconsciously, to a therapeutic technique, a consciousness-raising event. For others, prayer has lost its form as dialogue and address, becoming instead a mystical silence before one's Creator and Lord. Now, to be sure, confession will prove therapeutic for it will help us to face up to who we are. And prayer, even the prayer of confession, can have an appropriate and mystical silence as we come into the presence of our God. But neither the promise of therapy nor the possibility of silence will encourage the fervency of confession that characterizes Psalm 51. We confess because we must, as part of our ongoing relationship with our God. We confess because as we open ourselves in prayer to our God, acknowledging His glory, we are confronted with the *need* to confess. As we seek in prayer, in the words of Donald Bloesch, to take "hold of the outstretched hand of God," we confess. If we must confess to not confessing, could it be that we also are not praying?

Discussion Questions

1. Why is it that there are so few psalms of confession? And why have these taken such a prominent place in the church while other more plentiful laments have taken a backseat?

2. Must our prayers include confession with them?

3. Is Psalm 51 against the Old Testament sacrificial system?

4. How is the lament found in verses 3 through 5 unique among the many Psalms of Lament?

5. What is the nature of God as portrayed in this psalm?

6. For the psalmist, what does forgiveness entail?

7. Is there any sin that God cannot use for His glory?

Four

Psalm 80: When the Church Complains

(A Communal Lament)

Scripture records that in times of Israel's national crises, her people and leaders would come together to cry out to God for deliverance. When war or famine, or plague threatened, a fast would be proclaimed and all would assemble to seek help from God, to hear assurance of His care and to sing praises to His name. Solomon, in his prayer of dedication of the Temple, recognized the importance of these occasions of national lament and asked God to continue to intervene. We read in 1 Kings: "If there is famine in the land, if there is pestilence . . . if their enemy besieges them . . . whatever plague, whatever sickness there is; whatever prayer, whatever supplication is made by any man or by all thy people Israel . . . then hear thou in heaven thy dwelling place, and forgive, and act . . . that they may fear thee all the days that they live in the land which thou gavest to our fathers" (1 Kings 8:37-40).

Second Chronicles 20 records a specific instance of Solomon's request. King Jehoshaphat proclaims a

fast throughout Judah, for the armies of the Moab-
ites and the Ammonites threaten. The people gather
and cry out in distress, pleading with God to intervene. Then God raises up a prophet who speaks
words of assurance to them: "Fear not, and be not
dismayed; tomorrow go out against them, and the
Lord will be with you" (v. 17). Such assurance
changes the mood of the assembly drastically. They
now stand up and "praise the Lord, the God of Israel,
with a very loud voice" (v. 19).

The book of Joel describes a similar situation. A
locust plague is the occasion for Joel to call the whole
community to lament this situation and to plead to
the Lord (Joel 2:15-17). Israel's prayer leads Joel, in
turn, to declare as God's spokesperson that God has
answered Israel's cry. He is sending grain, wine and
oil (Joel 2:18-22). And this fact leads Joel to call the
people to rejoice in the Lord and to praise His name
(Joel 2:23-27). The pattern of address to God—
lament and petition—words of assurance—praise is
again apparent.

What is evident in these several descriptions of
Israel's national laments is that the chief characteristics of the lament of the individual (see chap. 2) have
been maintained, although the statements of assurance and the experience of praise now take place
beyond the strict confines of the lament itself. The
people come together to address Yahweh. They cry
out to Him with lament and petition, pleading with
Him in a variety of ways. They then sense His leading
and guiding, often through the proclamation of the
prophet (2 Chron. 20; Joel 2) or a priest (Ps. 12:5).
This, in turn, causes them to respond in praise.

It is this historical background and general pattern of lamentation that stand behind the Psalms of

the Communal Lament (Pss. 12; 44; 58; 60; 74; 79;
80; 83; 85; 90; 94; 106; 123; 126; 129; 137). Here is
the general historical-literary context for Psalm 80.

Psalm 80: A Communal Lament

The address (vv. 1,2). God is addressed in Psalm
80 as the "Shepherd of Israel" (v. 1). He is the one
who shines forth before Ephraim and Benjamin and
Manasseh. Such a nationalistically-oriented title for
God helps us understand the particular context in
which this psalm was no doubt composed. Samaria,
the capital of Israel, the Northern Kingdom, was in
the territory of Ephraim. Moreover, the tribes of
Ephraim and Manasseh dominated the center of the
region. They represent, therefore, the Northern Kingdom which is portrayed as in grave danger, about to
be swept away by Assyria. (It is interesting that the
Septuagint, the early Greek translation of the Old
Testament, adds to the title, "A Psalm Concerning
the Assyrian." The title is not part of the original
psalm, but it seems appropriate nonetheless.) God,
the God of Israel, the God of the Northern Kingdom,
the God of Joseph, He who has time after time rescued His people as a shepherd does His sheep, is
pleaded with. The time is close to 722 B.C., when
Israel will finally be taken captive. The time is that
period of the nation's slow death when hysteria and
suffering are on the increase and doom is imminent.

The introductory petition (vv. 2b,3). The psalmist
gets right to the point: "Stir up thy might, and come
to save us!" God's people are powerless; the help of
the Almighty is needed. To reinforce his request the
psalmist adds an additional sentence ("Restore us
. . ."), and this becomes the psalm's unifying refrain,
being repeated three times (vv. 3, 7, 19). Just as we

observed in our discussion of Psalm 51, the psalmist is not a slave to the typical form of a lament. Rather, the individuality of the writer shines through in this insertion of a refrain in an otherwise standard pattern of community lament. What is evident as well is the intensity of the psalmist's cry. For with each refrain, the songwriter enlarges the title of the God he addresses. In verse 3 he simply says "O God." In verse 7 he is calling upon the "God of hosts." And by the final refrain he is pleading with the "Lord God of hosts."

It is interesting to note that the phrase "restore us" might have an element of confession included in it. Certainly some of the other Psalms of Community Lament do (see Ps. 79:8,9). There is at the least a recognition by the psalmist that Israel is being judged by God (see Ps. 80:4). In the national disloyalty of Israel (see the book of Amos), something perhaps alluded to in verse 18 of our psalm, the writer recognizes the sin of God's people. The Assyrian threat is thus a spiritual judgment from God.

The complaint (vv. 4-6). The psalmist casts his lament in poetic terms. The only nourishment for God's people seems to be their own bitter tears, for they have become a laughingstock to others. There are again, as in the personal laments (see chap. 2), three actors involved in the situation: *God*, who is angry (v. 4); the *people*, who are in tears (v. 5); and their *enemies*, who laugh (v. 6). Yet the psalmist also recognizes that at a more fundamental level there is but one actor, God Himself. He is ultimately responsible. Thus the psalmist pleads throughout the psalm for God to pay attention ("give ear"; "let thy face shine"; "turn again"; "look down"; "see"; "have regard").

The request and reasons for action (vv. 8-16).
Having spelled out the dire situation, the psalmist
has (as is so often the case with these laments) a double wish. He pleads both for restoration for Israel and
for judgment upon her enemies: "Look down from
heaven and see; have regard for this vine . . . may
they perish at the rebuke of thy countenance!" (vv.
14-16) Restore us and defeat our adversary is the
two-sided plea. It is really just one plea—the flip sides
of the same coin. To make his people strong once
again will mean to rebuke the enemy of God's people
and cause them to perish. The one follows from the
other as night from day. Sometimes our contemporary notions of tolerance in a pluralistic society cause
us to ignore the interconnectedness of life. To ask for
certain things carries with it wider implications concerning others. The psalmist recognizes this and
boldly states the full implications of his plea.

The psalmist pleads for his people to be restored,
for they are a vineyard previously planted and tended
by God (vv. 8-11). In former days God had caused
them to flourish. Their vine had been so lush that
even the rugged mountains (where vines did not
often grow) were covered by its shade (v. 10). It had
become so strong even the mighty cedars were
eclipsed. Israel's vine covered the whole land, stretch-
ing from the Mediterranean Sea on the west to the
Euphrates River on the northeast (v. 11; see also
Deut. 11:24).

In light of God's former gracious activity, the
psalmist cries out on behalf of his people. "How can
you now, O God, let this vine be ravished and
burned? Yahweh, wake up" (Ps. 80:12-14; see also
Ps. 44:23). The contrast is here drawn as starkly as
possible between past prosperity and present hope-

lessness. This is perhaps the key element in most communal laments; it certainly functions in such a way here. Given their former glory and God's past blessing, the Israelites' present distress is even more lamentable. Some scholars have labeled this tension the "tragic reversal." There is perceived to be a movement from glory (vv. 8-11) to shame (vv. 12,13). No wonder the outcry! But the lament does not end here with the present distress, the apparent dashing of all hope.

The concluding vow of praise (vv. 17,18). Israel's faith insisted, instead, that God in His sovereignty would bring good out of ill. The final outcome would not be for God's people a slide from glory to shame, but a gracious reversal from shame to glory. We have noted that this confidence concerning God's steadfast mercy was the guiding force of the personal laments (see chap. 2 on Ps. 13). We have observed above in our discussion of both 2 Chronicles 20 and Joel 2 that this movement from lament to praise and trust oftentimes took place beyond the confines of the psalm—in the dialogue of worship as the prophet or priest represented God to His people and spoke words of assurance. But even in some of the psalms of communal complaint themselves there is evidence of Israel's trust in the God of grace. In verse 17 of Psalm 80, the psalmist looks forward to God's deliverance. The language is tentative, being expressed in the subjunctive form ("let . . ."). But the psalmist's faith in God is evident. "The son of man" (Israel) has been made strong (past tense) by his God (v. 17; see also vv. 8,9). The writer looks forward to Israel's future salvation when this will again be the case. Then the nation will again call on God's name, praising Him in His Temple (v. 18; see also Ps. 79:13).

Conclusion

What can we conclude from our study of this psalm? Four related subjects suggest themselves.

First, protest is not for the sake of protesting. Israel's laments in the Psalms are never an end in themselves, never merely getting it off one's chest. They are, rather, even in their most extreme form, an appeal for help and an anticipation of God's saving intervention. A minister I know used to frustrate his congregation by responding to their complaints, "Thanks for telling me that. It is important for us to know where we stand with each other and for you to be able to express yourself." Although that no doubt was true, it was not a helpful response. The congregation wanted action, not just catharsis—a wrestling with the problem, not merely recognition of its existence. Such is the case with Israel as well. Her laments are neither monologue nor therapy nor mere descriptions. They are appeals for help with the expectation that God will respond.

Second, it is important to notice here the corporate dimension of Israel's faith. Many of Israel's psalms are laments of the individual. But there are also laments of the nation, as we observe here in Psalm 80. Neither the individual nor the community is lost sight of in Israel. Both are controlled by God and are in need of His grace.

As a society and as a church (particularly the Protestant church), we in the West have lost this dual focus and have become one-sidedly individualistic. In the church, as Dietrich Bonhoeffer noted so forcefully in his *Letters and Papers from Prison*, we have asked only such questions as "Are you (the individual) going to heaven?" and "Are you (the individual) working industriously and honestly in your voca-

tion?" These are vital questions and are not to be
ignored. They are at one pole of the Christian experience.

But where is the place among God's people for the
corporate cry of the oppressed? Where is the sense of
corporate solidarity among God's people? This too
should find central expression in our life of faith. We
should not only cry, "Save *me.*" We can and must also
cry, "Save *us.*" Examples of this need are easily found
even today. One thinks of the plea that was made by
God's people worldwide for the church in Uganda
under Idi Amin. One thinks as well of the expression
of anguish and faith coming out of many of the Third
World (less developed) countries today. What of the
church in El Salvador? or in Honduras? In the face of
epidemics and widespread malnutrition, in the face
of intractable poverty, in the face of wars and famine,
the church worldwide should be crying out collec-
tively. But are we? Do we in North America share the
bond of common concern? Will we join in the
anguished cry of our brothers and sisters in need?

The title or superscription of Psalm 80 is significant, though it is not a part of the original inspired
Scripture; for the title identifies the psalm as a "Testimony of Asaph." Asaph was a court musician in
David's day (see 1 Chron. 16:7) and his name came to
be associated with a guild of singers at the second
Temple (Neh. 7:44). Thus it is probable that the composer of this psalm, living in the period between
David and Nehemiah, was from Jerusalem, not
Samaria where the suffering was currently being
experienced. Here we have the heartfelt cry of one of
God's people living in Judah for his brothers and sisters in Samaria. We cannot prove this with certainty,
but it is likely that Psalm 80 is a model of corporate

solidarity with others in their time of need. Judah is praying for Israel. Are we praying as earnestly for suffering Christians in other churches and lands?

Third, Israel's faith in God allowed her to protest boldly to Him. Even the absurd is brought before God. There is no meek submissiveness here, no downplaying the agony and hurt because of a false sense of respect. The psalmist does not say, "If it is thy will, O Lord," or, "Have thy own way, Lord." That is assumed. God will accomplish His purposes. In fact, this recognition of God's sovereignty is what triggers the complaint. God will do as He wills. The psalmist only wants to affect God's will—to challenge Him to a new course of action. The psalmist wants God to "repent" (see also Jonah 3:10; Exod. 32:14).

God is faithful to His character. He is unchangeable. His actions are consistent with His nature. But part of His nature is to respond like a mother to the needs of her children (or to change the metaphor, like a shepherd to the distress of his sheep, Ps. 80:1). It is the recognition that God cares for us and responds to our cries that allows this psalmist the freedom of honest protest. All the cards are laid out on the table so that God can respond.

It is worth noting the central place of protest in the life of God's people, the Israelites. Protest seems presumptuous to many sincere Christians today. But notice these Psalms of Lament. And recall the central place historically of the corporate complaint in Israel's life. For example, Moses concludes his address to his people at the end of his life by quoting an early "creed," reciting what God's people believed and should believe. He tells them, This is what you should say to the Lord: "A wandering Aramean was my father; and he went down into Egypt . . . and there he became a nation, great, mighty, and populous. And the Egyptians treated us harshly. . . . Then we cried to the Lord the God of our fathers, and the Lord heard our voice, and saw our affliction, our toil, and our oppression; and the Lord brought us out of Egypt . . . and gave us this land, a land flowing with milk and honey. And behold, now I bring the first of the fruit of the ground, which thou, O Lord, hast given me" (Deut. 26:5-10).

The Israelites were mighty; they became oppressed; they cried out in agony and protest; God rescued them; they were given a land; they are now to thank the Lord. Does the pattern, the progression, sound familiar? It should, for this is the *very* pattern of the laments of the Psalms. We will comment on the significance of this fact later, but first it is important to observe within this early creed the prominence given to the complaint of God's people in their time of need.

God is a God who responds to our cries of need. He does this, Israel came to realize, even when their cry lacked total sincerity or trust. Recall the murmurings of the Israelites in the wilderness (Exod. 16:1-3). The response to their protest is God's gracious raining down bread and quail for food. Moses tells his people, You have murmured against the Lord. But he has heard your cry and said: "At twilight you shall eat flesh, and in the morning you shall be filled with bread; then you shall know that I am the Lord your God" (Exod. 16:12). In Isaiah we find a second example. Although the protest has turned cynical and faithless, Isaiah proclaims that God's understanding and love is unsearchable and ever abounding. He gives power to the faint so that they can "run and not be weary" (Isa. 40:27-31). Isaiah preached such a message of hope for his people and for us.

Fourth, Israel's cry of protest and complaint figures prominently within Old Testament faith. The lament is, in fact, a central paradigm or model by which the life of God's people is described. Israel prospers because of God's grace; Israel's fortunes reverse (because of sin); Israel cries out in need; Yahweh hears and acts; Israel reacts in praise. This is the pattern, as we have observed, of Moses' early creed (Deut. 26:5-10). It is the pattern of the Exodus event and the book of Judges. It is the pattern by which the monarchy is remembered (1 and 2 Kings). It is even the pattern in the New Testament used to describe Peter's attempt to walk on the water (Matt. 14:29-33).

God is a God who responds to the needs of His people. Our requests *are* important, as this basic paradigm of biblical faith attests. The prayer of God's people is crucial to their well-being. If we are as a church in a period of growing secularization and crisis, could it be that we are not "complaining" passionately? When have we felt such emotion as did the psalmist of Psalm 80? or the Israelite in bondage in Egypt? or the Israelite in need of a judge? or Jeremiah as his nation faced impending doom? Israel finds her source of confidence in the pattern of God's response to His people's cries. Yahweh is not like the other gods, deaf and dumb. Instead, God is an answering God. As God says through His prophet Isaiah, "Before they call I will answer, while they are yet speaking I will hear" (Isa. 65:24).

A Postscript

This psalm of Israel was later applied by Jesus to Himself, the true Israel. He is the "Son of Man"; He is the true "vine." The Lord was steeped in the psalms.

As He spoke of His ministry He used them, including Psalm 80, to identify Himself and His mission. Just as Israel was God's representative to the world, so Jesus was God's ultimate representative. Just as Israel was chosen to deal with the sin of the world, so Jesus was God's full solution. Just as Israel experienced God's judgment for her sin, so Jesus took upon Himself on the cross the sins of us all. And just as Israel experienced the gracious restoring hand of God, so Jesus arose from the dead. What was true of Israel in part was found to be true also of Jesus, only now in a perfect sense. In expressing this fact, both Jesus and the New Testament writers found in the psalms descriptions applicable to our Lord.

Discussion Questions

1. Should the church bear its suffering patiently? When is it permissible for it to *complain* to God?

2. In Christian worship, why has the lament faded from the position of prominence which it had in Israel's worship? Why are there so few songs, for example, in our hymnals that are laments or were inspired by the Psalms of Lament?

3. What Old Testament accounts relate the importance of crying out to God corporately in our time of need?

4. Compare Psalm 74 with Psalm 80 to find a similar pattern of national lament: the address (74:1), together with a recounting of God's past deeds (74:2), an introductory petition (74:2,3), the complaint (74:4-11), followed by a lengthier petition for God to intervene and reasons given as to why God should do this (74:12-23). What is missing? What explanation might be offered for this difference?

5. The imagery of the "vine" that is used here

seems to be the context out of which Jesus said, "I am the true vine" (John 15:1). Other Old Testament passages relating to a vineyard are Isaiah 5:1-7 and Ezekiel 15. Why do they not seem appropriate as a source for Jesus' use of the term to describe Himself?

6. When is the last time your church as a church protested to God?

Five

Psalm 137: Confronting an Evil World

(An Imprecatory Psalm)

It seems to be part of human nature to want to strike back when hurt. The situation in America's recent past when her hostages were returned from Iran is a particularly forceful example of this fact; for the public mood, fed both by the media and by government announcements, threatened to become angry.

Particularly enraged was former President Carter, as he stood at the U. S. Air Base in Frankfurt, Germany, emotionally and physically drained by the negotiations and bitter that the joy of a triumphant close to his presidency had been denied him, seemingly out of malice. He denounced the Iranian captors as "terrorists" who had committed "a despicable act of savagery" which, he said, "will never be forgotten." And later in his handwritten report to the new president he wrote, "Never do any favors for the hoodlums who persecuted innocent American heroes." They are "animals, almost."

Similar expressions of hatred which were voiced

by some of the hostages concerning their captors had a certain black humor. One prisoner wanted to give them not cash but "eight billion dollars worth of bombs," and another commented dryly, "I hope Allah *never* answers their prayers."

Such animosity spread quickly across much of the United States, threatening for a time to engulf us. From the obscene bumper stickers on automobiles to the *Wall Street Journal* editorial suggesting that we fail to honor our word in the negotiated settlement, many Americans sought ways to retaliate, to lash out. Frustration abounded as feelings of vengeance surfaced.

It is against a similar backdrop of earlier glory, of national humiliation, and of backlash against terrorism that Psalm 137 was set. Like many today the psalmist longed for those days when his country had been strong and prosperous. Like some today he cried out for revenge against his enemies, against Babylon his present captor, and against Edom who helped the Babylonians sack Jerusalem in 587 B.C. (Obad. 10—14; 2 Kings 25:8-12). And like at least some who cry out today, the psalmist used shocking language, expressive of extreme emotion and even hatred. But is the psalmist also to be judged as giving in to that most common of human sins—the desire to get back at those who hurt us?

How are we to understand this psalm in our Bibles? Can vengeance ever be justified? Most of us were rightly embarrassed by the extremism of some seeking vengeance against Iran. How can the psalmist adopt a posture that seems so similar? Would we ever be justified in praying such a psalm as this? The questions rush forth, and they are not new. Psalm 137 has puzzled Christians through the centuries, and the situation in Iran only helps to focus our attention once again on one of the more vexing problems of interpretation in our Bibles, the question of vengeance expressed in the psalms. What does the hatred found in Psalm 137 have to do with us today, particularly in the light of God's further revelation in Jesus Christ?

C. S. Lewis, in a well-known chapter in his *Reflections on the Psalms*, expressed the opinion that although vindictive hatred appears in the Bible it is not good or pious. It is "profoundly natural," he says, but also "profoundly wrong." He compares the situation to that of English soldiers fighting the Nazi regime in World War II and calls the bitter personal vindictiveness "a good symptom, though bad in itself," for "it is a sin." "If the Jews cursed more bitterly than the Pagans," he reasons, "this was . . . at least in part because they took right and wrong more seriously." Lewis concludes his discussion by saying, "The ferocious parts of the Psalms serve as a reminder that there is in the world such a thing as wickedness and that it (if not its perpetrators) is hateful to God. In that way, however dangerous the human distortion may be, (God's) word sounds through these passages too."

Lewis's conclusion that hateful vengeance is obviously wrong and therefore God's Word must be seen as having been filtered through human distortion and sin seems unacceptable to those holding to the full inspiration and trustworthiness of Scripture, of God's-Word-as-human-words. It is a self-defeating principle of interpretation to juxtapose God's Word as pure with the Bible's human words as sometimes sinful. But if the expressions of vengeance heard in the Psalms cause the usually-reliable Lewis to fall into error, how then can we escape the same snare? How is it that vengeance can ever be a human virtue? In answering this question we need to turn to Psalm 137 itself for answers.

Psalm 137: A National Lament

Psalm 137 is another of Israel's Psalms of Communal Lament, similar to Psalm 80, which we studied in chapter 4. It is, however, not an altogether typical one.

The introduction (vv. 1,2). Where many of the other national laments in the Psalms begin by addressing God, by first invoking His name (see Ps. 60, "O God"; Ps. 80, "Give ear, O Shepherd of Israel"), Psalm 137 begins more introspectively. The psalmist immediately relates the story of his sorry circumstances. It is almost as though the extremity of his situation causes him to forego the usual situation.

The complaint (vv. 3,4). The psalmist is a captive during the Babylonian exile where the prisoners of war are being ridiculed by their captors. They are told to sing some of their psalms of Zion for the captors' enjoyment. (Perhaps these songs of Zion are ones like Psalms 46, 48, 84, and 122.) But this is impossible, for Zion now lies in ashes. To lightly sing its praise is a mockery; it is unthinkable. It is not merely the personal humiliation involved. Rather, the holiness of God is being profaned. The psalmist will not cast his pearls before swine.

The statement of trust (vv. 4-6). As the psalm proceeds, the psalmist turns from plaintively spilling out his distress to stubbornly confessing his continuing loyalty to Jerusalem—to the city of God—and thus indirectly to God Himself. Jerusalem's disaster and his present torment only reinforce the psalmist's determination to defy his captors. (He will only give name, rank, and serial number!) He will not allow Zion to be ridiculed. Better that his tongue be permanently silenced.

The petition (vv. 7-9). Having described the present situation and affirmed his resolve to remain faithful to Zion and her God, the author recalls the day of Jerusalem's destruction when Edom joined Babylon in acts of atrocity. Overcome with grief and indignation he cries out to God to judge his persecutors in kind and destroy them. The language is judicial. ("Remember . . . against" was a phrase rooted in the legal procedures of ancient Israel.) God, the divine Judge, has been reminded of the evidence by the psalmist. God's people are faithful (vv. 4-6); God's enemies, faithless (vv. 1-3). Therefore a "guilty" verdict is in order. Justice must be affirmed. As Edom and Babylon acted outrageously and vengefully in the day of Jerusalem's destruction (see Ezek. 25:12-17; Obad. 11—14), so the psalmist pleads with God to respond outrageously. "An eye for an eye," a baby for a baby; here is how God's honor can be preserved.

This, then, is the psalm. What can we learn from it? As the psalm reaches its violent and shocking climax, most of us feel very uncomfortable. And this is understandable in the light of God's further revelation which we have received. But before we look at this psalm in its larger New Testament context, it is important to hear its message from God to us on its own terms. How can the psalm's cry be understood? How can it be appropriated by us? What is God's message to us in Psalm 137?

God's Message to Us

Let me summarize four lessons we can learn from

this psalm—lessons concerning ways we can respond appropriately to the *evil* we encounter.

Focus upon God. A starting point comes as we notice the natural progression of the hymn. The songwriter does not begin with his cry for vengeance; he ends there. It is only after expressing his lament to God, only after declaring his continuing trust in God and his commitment to Zion, God's chosen city, that the psalmist is inspired to cry for vengeance against the Lord's (and therefore, his) enemies. It is not self-pity or personal rancor or self-centered pride that motivates him. (Those are the motives most apt to inspire our own cries for revenge.) But it is the fact of God's righteousness that calls forth his imprecation. The focus of the lament is on *God* and His people; upon *God* and His place, Jerusalem; upon *God* and His enemies. We will return to consider who this God is in a later paragraph, but here we note first of all that evil is judged with reference to *God*. If we are tempted to use Psalm 137 as justification for our own feelings of vengeance and judgment, let us be sure we are motivated only by our love for God, not merely by regard for ourselves.

Be willing to express shock. The psalmist's outrage at evil, at the indignity his God is enduring (not merely the indignity the writer is experiencing) causes him to scream. We are so jaded, so civilized that nothing much shocks us today, and what does shock us we suppress. Not so the psalmist. His feelings of horror at the present evil well up within him as he moves from pathos (vv. 1-3), through stubborn resolve (vv. 4-6), to open hatred (vv. 7-9). Mere description of the situation is insufficient. Language of the heart is called for. The psalmist's words are meant to awaken us, as they awaken God, to a full awareness of the extremity of evil. Given the godless ridicule of the enemy, the psalmist must express his desperation in the strongest language possible. Again, how different his reaction is from our own. How willing are we to let evil upset our equilibrium? Or do we insulate ourselves in our polite civility?

Address the here and now. Along with the psalmist's understanding of evil with reference to God, not to himself, and along with his willingness to be truly *shocked* by such evil, it must be remembered that in the psalmist's day, God's progressive revelation to humankind was still incomplete (not defective, just incomplete, partial). We now know more of God's nature and will because of Jesus Christ than this psalmist did. In particular we have a sure hope that divine justice carries beyond death and will be once and for all achieved at the final judgment. The good news of Jesus' death and resurrection is in part the fact that death is not the end and God's ultimate vindication is assured. But such a perspective was unknown to this psalmist.

Throughout the Old Testament the Israelites evidenced little awareness of life beyond the grave. (Daniel is the exception, but its perspectives do not seem to have influenced other Old Testament writings.) The few allusions and affirmations concerning life after death which are found in the Old Testament are the inspired projections of God-fearing individuals concerning the nature of God's faithfulness to them (see Ps. 73:26; Job 19:26). Given the extent of God's steadfastness and love, a few were able to express the firm belief that death would not intrude on their relationship with God. But such highpoints of faith are rare and are not generalized into an overall doctrine of immortality until the Hellenistic period.

For the Old Testament person, if justice is to prevail, it must be achieved here and now, in this life, for only Sheol awaits. There is throughout the Psalms a matter-of-fact acceptance of death as the end. (Ps. 6:4,5 states: "Turn, O Lord, save my life. . . . For in death there is no remembrance of thee; in Sheol who can give thee praise?" See also Ps. 90:1-10.)

Given the lack of perspective on an afterlife and the concentration on one's life as a child of God in the here-and-now, is it any wonder that the psalmist's cries take on an urgency? If God does not act now, God's honor will be compromised. If Babylon and Edom are not punished here and now, God will be thought impotent to save His people.

It is important for us to let the psalmist's concern for the present teach us. There is a tension in the Christian life between the present and the future, between the Kingdom of God here and now and the Kingdom yet to be. We know that in Christ evil has been vanquished. Nevertheless, the total defeat of evil yet waits. This tension is meant to be creative and must be maintained. It is meant to strengthen our present opposition to evil, even while protecting us from disillusionment and cynicism.

Too often we flee into the future in our thinking. We disregard present reality. We say, "There will always be wars," and fail to let our outrage against evil work for present peace. We believe that the malnourished, the weak, the poor can one day find rest with the Lord, and this blunts our indignation over present injustice. Not so for the psalmist. Evil must be rooted out *now*. Here is a third perspective from Psalm 137 which we need to integrate into our own lives.

Uphold God's justice (and grace). The lessons

concerning evil which Psalm 137 can teach us are several. First, as we encounter evil we should focus our attention on God, not merely on ourselves. Second, it is right that we allow ourselves to be shocked by evil. Again, we must not undercut our present action against evil by fleeing to the safety of heaven's final accounting. Third, God calls us also to be His agents in redeeming the time in the present situation. Fourth, the psalm instructs us concerning God's *justice*, concerning His response to evil.

In Deuteronomy 7:9,10 we read: "Know therefore that the Lord your God is God, the faithful God who keeps covenant and steadfast love with those who love him and keep his commandments, to a thousand generations, and requites to their face those who hate him, by destroying them; he will not be slack with him who hates him, he will requite him to his face."

Here is the psalmist's perspective. God declares Himself through the words of Moses as being in a covenant relationship with His people. Within the terms of that relationship, moreover, He will act as Judge and Vindicator to uphold justice. He will requite the enemy to his face. It is because God has promised the vindication of His people that the psalmist cries out. It is not presumption on his part, but faithfulness to God's word that motivates the writer of the psalm.

Given the godless enemy, the salvation of God's people involves the certainty of destruction of those who hate Him. And vice versa. To our ears, vindication carries the echoes of pride and spitefulness. But to the Hebrew ear, accustomed to such words as those in Deuteronomy 7, it carried the broader implication of God's salvation. (It is interesting to note that one of the Hebrew words for vengeance, *naqam*, has as its root or basic meaning, "to save.") Are we who are so conditioned to be tolerant and open in our attitudes, even regarding evil, willing to recognize that God's judgment upon evil is the opposite side of His loving-kindness toward those who love Him? God's justice cannot be divorced from His grace.

Justice and Grace

Some will deny that this cry of the psalmist could incorporate within it a sense of God's graciousness. How can the sufferings of innocents ever be included within an understanding of God's grace? The smashing of babies' heads is beyond our imagination. However, this was not the case in the ancient world. The practice seems to have been a common one among Israel's victorious neighbors (see 2 Kings 8:12; Isa. 13:16; Hos. 10:14; 13:16; it also has its modern equivalent in some of the World War II concentration camps). In calling for God to dash the little ones against a rock, the psalmist is asking not for the exceptional by way of punishment, but for the *comparable*. The barbarism connected with Jerusalem's fall must be answered in kind, as the Law advised: "If any harm follows, then you shall give life for life, eye for eye, tooth for tooth, hand for hand, foot for foot, burn for burn, wound for wound, stripe for stripe" (Exod. 21:23-25; see also Lev. 24:20; Deut. 19:21).

Such a principle of retribution, spiteful as it might seem in our context, had a gracious as well as a righteous intention. God desired that evil be purged out and feared. He also desired His people to *limit* all punishment to that which was appropriate to the offense. In contrast to the excesses of other ancient Near Eastern peoples, God declared, "An eye for an eye; no more!" The psalmist, thus, even at the height of his passion, remains true to his God, a God both of justice and of grace. He asks for retributive justice, no less, but also no more.

A New Testament Perspective

In the Sermon on the Mount, Jesus extended the Old Testament teaching concerning retributive justice. He declared: "You have heard that it was said, 'An eye for an eye and a tooth for a tooth.' But I say to you, Do not resist one who is evil. But if anyone strikes you on the right cheek, turn to him the other also" (Matt. 5:38,39).

Does this contradict the lessons we have learned from this psalm concerning evil? No. Does this mean that evil is no longer shocking or an affront to God? No. However, given God's further revelation of divine grace, we can no longer pray for justice to be administered in the way the writer of Psalm 137 did. We can learn about evil from his inspired words; we can learn of God's hatred of wrongdoing; we can be challenged to oppose present injustice; we can realize more fully that in God's character justice (judgment) and love (mercy) are united. But we must also learn to love not hate our enemies. Ultimately, God's mercy, and ours, must prevail even over evil.

Paul, accepting the authority of both the Old Testament and Jesus' teaching, gives us a Christian approach to vengeance in the twelfth chapter of Romans. We are to bless our persecutors and refrain from pride. We are not to repay evil for evil, Paul admonishes, but to live at peace with all if possible. God's honor will be vindicated, but that is for Him to accomplish, not us. And God in His grace has chosen to forbear for yet a time, to remain patient, so that all might repent and believe. Rather than seek vengeance, however justified it might be, the Christian community must instead seek "to overcome evil with good" (Rom. 12:9-21).

A Final Postscript

Let me, in closing, return briefly to the feelings of some regarding the Iranian captors. Were those who were calling for retribution justified? What has our Psalm taught us?

1. Evil, whether in this country or Iran, is abhorrent to God and should be so identified by His people. Moreover, it should be shocking to us. One must be sure, however, that his or her outrage is against what is evil in God's sight and not merely against our personal humiliation.

2. God's vengeance against those who are enemies of His people cannot serve to validate judgment against an enemy of the United States. We are not, as a nation, God's chosen, special people. Rather, it is God's people, the church, which functions in a similar capacity today.

3. Was the cry of outrage against Iran because God's honor was attacked, because His justice needed affirming, or because our pride of person and country had been challenged? The psalmist's cry for retribution involved God and His people, God and His enemies. It is this divine focus that controlled the psalmist and which should control us.

4. Lastly, Psalm 137 teaches that vengeance is of God, not us. The psalmist cries out for God to act. And in His own time and way, act He did—in the person of Jesus Christ. Although the Babylonians were never terribly punished (they fell to Persia with little bloodshed), God answered the psalmist's prayer by taking on Himself the Babylonians' deserved punish-

ment, dying in a horrible way on the cross. In this way God's justice was demonstrated, but so too His grace.

Paul, having experienced the wonder of the cross of Jesus Christ, recognizes that in that event God intervened decisively against evil, yet graciously. Justice was affirmed, and yet mercy was demonstrated. It is in the light of Jesus Christ and His cross that Paul responds to the question concerning vengeance in our day by saying, Vengeance is *God's* business, not ours. " 'If your enemy is hungry, feed him; if he is thirsty, give him drink; for by so doing you will heap burning coals upon his head.' Do not be overcome by evil, but overcome evil with good" (Rom. 12:20,21).

Discussion Questions

1. What is the historical background of this psalm?

2. Why is it so important to the psalmist that God deal with His enemies now?

3. In what way does the Old Testament standard of "an eye for an eye" reflect both God's justice and His mercy?

4. Should the Psalter be "censored" at those points which offend us? (See Pss. 139:19-22; 109:1,2; 69:22-28.) How does the New Testament add further light on these texts?

5. Why is it inadequate to say that in Psalm 137 the writer gave in (in v. 9) to "human passion" after earnestly striving to honor God and to be faithful to Him?

6. How might the discussion in this chapter be applied to the cry of the psalmist in Psalm 109:6-19?

Six

Psalm 23: Responding to Crisis

(A Psalm of Trust)

The film *The Elephant Man* is based loosely on the true story of John Merrick, a hideously deformed young man who lived in the 1880s, during the time of England's industrial revolution. Known in the circus sideshows as the Elephant Man, Merrick was thought to be an idiot, incapable of feeling or speech. He lived a cruel, demeaning life until rescued by Sir Frederick Treves of the London Hospital.

Treves, a lecturer in anatomy at the Medical College, first saw Merrick as a "specimen" to analyze, but his compassion for John grew daily. Hiding Merrick in an isolation ward of the hospital, Treves sought to care for him. However, hospital policy did not permit "incurables" to be admitted permanently, for space was limited. Thus, Carr Gomm, the hospital administrator, asked Treves to show him the deformed man so that he could evaluate whether Merrick was capable of being helped. Central to the decision was whether the young man could think and speak as a normal person.

In a moving sequence of the film Sir Frederick Treves goes to John and pleads with him to show Treves that he has intelligence. "I can't help you unless you help me. I believe there is something you want to say to me. . . . I have to understand what you are thinking and feeling. We must show them that you're not a wall." Finally, sensing that Treves wants to help him, John tentatively responds. Treves now knows that Merrick is a normal person apart from his physical deformities and begins a crash course to prepare him to meet the hospital administrator who is to decide his fate. Among the sentences which Merrick practices repeating after Treves are the first three verses of the twenty-third Psalm.

At two in the afternoon on the following day Treves, Carr Gomm and John Merrick meet. The administrator asks John simple questions, but although he can respond his answers seem to be by rote. Somewhat cynically Carr Gomm asks, "How long did you and Mr. Treves prepare for this interview?" Merrick, sensing he has failed, cannot respond adequately. Carr Gomm has heard enough. He turns to leave and, as Treves and the administrator pause in the hall after closing the door behind him, they hear John Merrick begin to recite the twenty-third Psalm. This time, however, John does not merely echo Treves. He continues the psalm beyond what his mentor has taught him, saying ever more forcefully, "Yea, though I walk through the valley of the shadow of death, I will fear no evil; for Thou art with me."

Hearing John Merrick articulate this radical affirmation of trust in God, Treves realizes he has not taught that part of the psalm to Merrick. He persuades Carr Gomm to return to the room where they learn from John, who is now calm enough to speak, that his mother had taught him the psalm as a child. It is in this way that his crisis is solved. Sensitive, intelligent, and appreciative of even the smallest of favors, John becomes to all who meet him a model of what true humanity is.

The film *The Elephant Man* is an eloquent witness to the original intention and meaning of Psalm 23, for the psalm is a cry to God in a time of great need. The simplicity of its imagery and the peacefulness of its message have made the psalm a favorite of believers. It is often repeated in a variety of circumstances. But what needs to be understood is that Psalm 23 is not a general affirmation of faith by someone reflecting on his life. It is not a psalm written when all is well and God seems near at hand. Rather, it is the poetic cry of one shaken, one in the midst of danger, one in need of help. It is a psalm for us to sing when crisis threatens.

Psalm 23: A Psalm of Trust

We know that Psalm 23 was written in crisis (and for our crises), for its "form" is a variation on the Psalms of Individual Lament which we have already studied in chapter 2. In our study of Psalm 13, we noted that the author expressed his cry to God in time of need by using a typical outline for such songs—an order which began with an opening address (Ps. 13:1a), followed by a complaint (13:1,2), a petition with reasons for acting (13:3,4), a confession of trust (13:5), and a vow to again praise God (13:6). It is this confession of trust, so typical of the personal lament (see also Ps. 7:10-16; 9:3-12), that the psalmist has here expanded into an entire psalm.

Rather than call out to God for help, or recount

his distress, or seek to persuade the Lord to intervene, the psalmist is content to sing a song of confidence in his Lord. Such an approach to crisis is not
unique in the Psalter, although Psalm 23 stands
alone in its power and poetry. Other Psalms of Trust
include Psalms 11, 16, and 62. In Psalm 11, for
example, we hear that the psalmist has taken refuge
in the Lord (v. 1). But rather than explain his situation or lament his plight, the writer sings a song of
trust to his God! Again, Psalm 16 begins with the cry,
"Preserve me, O God, for in thee I take refuge." But
before we can learn anything more of the threat with
which he is faced, the songwriter is caught up in
devotion to his God for the remainder of the psalm.
Psalm 62 mentions enemies who curse the psalmist,
but here too the focus is not on the author's plight,
but on God, his hope and salvation.

In the Psalms of Trust, of which Psalm 23 is the
best known, the context in which they are written is
one of oppression and distrust. Each of the psalmists
is in need of help. But in every case, the writer's
response is not a request for assistance but a positive
affirmation of God's *hesed* (His mercy and steadfast
love) for His own.

> For God alone my soul waits in silence;
> > from him comes my salvation.
> He only is my rock and my salvation,
> > my fortress; I shall not be greatly
> > moved.

> > > (Ps. 62:1,2)

John Merrick, the suffering, deformed man, in
his hour of grave danger responded by praying Psalm
23. In so doing he was following the original author's
purpose and meaning. He was using Psalm 23 as it
was intended to be sung. In times of distress, the

writer of this psalm invites us to join with him in
singing a song of trust in the Lord.

A Psalm for the Whole Person

Psalm 23 expresses its radical faith in the Lord in
a time of need through the use of two central images.
God is portrayed as both the *good shepherd* and the
gracious host. The psalmist is not trying to fill our
minds with "facts" about God, although what he
sings is true. He is not trying to argue himself or his
readers into a sense of peace and contentment.
Rather, he seeks to fill his mind and ours with an
awareness of the wonder and glory of God.

David goes back to the time of his youth when he
was carefree and without any crises in his life. There
he finds, in his shepherding experiences and in the
Near Eastern customs of hospitality practiced by his
family, effective analogies, striking word pictures of
his God. He invites us to use these same images to
meditate with him on God and His ways. He would
have us be filled with an appreciation of the goodness
and the loving-kindness of God.

In chapter 1 we noted that the psalms are poetry.
They are meant to challenge the whole person—
mind, emotion, and will. Too often we exist in the
acid soil of the mind alone, content to analyze and
objectify. Psalm 23 invites its readers instead to
admire and to adore. It calls on us to approach our
God with wonder—to continuously delight in His love
and graciousness, to marvel at His abundant provision and incomparable goodness.

Before turning directly to the two metaphors—the
two word pictures used by the psalmist—it will be
helpful to reflect on the nature of the analogies which
are used in Psalm 23. Has the psalmist observed how

good shepherds act or hospitable hosts serve, and then projected these images upon his God? The answer surely is, no. David would find no ultimate assurance in time of need if he were simply creating a God in his own idealized image. And neither would we. David's God is not the projection of his imagination. Such analogies would only trivialize God and open their author to disappointment. God is not made in our image; we are made in *His*.

We do not whisper "God" by shouting "man," as Karl Barth once said. Rather, we must shout "God," and find in such revelation a whisper concerning ourselves. Here is the psalmist's approach. Because God is all goodness and grace we can know that our lives will be filled with goodness and grace. In his crisis, David turns to his God who reveals His nature to be like that of a good shepherd and a gracious host.

The Lord is my Shepherd. In the image of the shepherd we have one of the most meaningful and comprehensive word pictures of God in the psalms. In other psalms God is portrayed as a rock or shield or king; that is, God's glory and strength are graphically represented. But in the metaphor of the shepherd, it is not only God's strong protection that is highlighted, but also His continuing care. Not only is His majesty represented, but also His grace. (In the next chapter we will study Psalm 8 which describes further these complementary characteristics of our God.) God, the great God of the universe, is "my shepherd." The contrast is simple and yet profound. *God* is presented as *my* God, one who cares for me.

As the psalmist finds in what he knows of shepherding a suitable analogy for what he knows of God, he pictures God's care as being expressed in three ways: God, the shepherd, provides; He leads; and He protects. There is a natural progression in this development as the shepherd first meets the immediate needs of his "sheep" and then continues to provide by leading them along right paths into new pastures and by protecting them from harm by His presence. Try to paint a picture in your mind of this good shepherd as I describe Him.

First, God provides. Rather than feed amidst dry sagebrush thrusting out of arid soil, or grow hungry wandering among the rocky terrain of much of Judah's countryside, God's sheep feed in "green pastures." The setting is so lush that the animals are portrayed as having their appetites fully satisfied. They are content to lie down. Moreover, sheep desire still, rather than running, water to drink, and God the shepherd leads them to such a place. Whether He has dammed a small brook, as was common practice among shepherds, or instead has searched out an appropriate spot, we don't know. What is important to the sheep is not the how but the what. Water has been supplied. The result is refreshment and restoration. Because the shepherd provides food, there is no need to suffer want. Because he furnishes drink, his flock is restored. All the necessities and comfort that his sheep could desire are provided.

David, in his crisis, dwells upon God's character as provider. Having experienced God's fullness in days past, he can assert—despite the seeming evidence to the contrary—that God, his shepherd, will certainly provide for all his needs.

Secondly, *God leads.* The portrayal of God as shepherd-provider is the central metaphor of this Psalm of Trust. And God continues to provide by leading us. In the psalmist's day, pasture was scarce and food easily depleted. Thus the shepherd had to take his sheep on a continuous journey from place to place in search of provisions.

In portraying God as a shepherd who leads, David declares also why God is interested in directing us, His sheep. A question that many have concerning the Judeo-Christian God is how we can presume to think that the great God of the universe would care for us, would be interested in personally leading us. How could we think ourselves worthy of such concern? Aren't we too sinful and/or insignificant for God's nurturing grace, for God to lead us? Psalm 23 provides a clear answer and, in the process, increases our hope in time of need. For it states that God's guidance is "for his name's sake," not ours alone. The Shepherd-God leads, not because of who we, the sheep, are, but because of who He is—a shepherd.

"For his name's sake" stands for all that God is and does. David Hubbard suggests that the simplest paraphrase is to say "for his glory" (see Exod. 33:18-20). God provides for our needs and leads us along right paths so that He can reveal to men and angels alike who He is—namely, a God of steadfast love. Let me quote Hubbard again: "In all that God does, his own reputation is at stake. He will not let himself down. This is an assuring word. Our welfare, our security, our salvation, our destiny do not hinge on our ability. God has pledged himself to be our God in every sense of the word, and he will not back away from his commitment."[1]

God reveals Himself to be our shepherd. His character, His personality (for that is what one's "name" signifies in biblical thought) is that of a gracious provider and leader. Thus, even if we are but lowly sheep, God's shepherding rests not in who we are, but in who He is. It is in His nature to lead us in the paths of righteousness.

Thirdly, *God protects*. As the shepherd leads his flock into new pastures, he also protects them. So too our God. Through dark and treacherous valleys where death seems imminent, the shepherd watches over his sheep. With rod (or club) to ward off predators, and staff (or crook) to guide and restrain his sheep, the shepherd keeps his flock safe from harm. All the tools necessary, all the means possible to war against evil and to protect against calamity are at his command. God, the shepherd, will protect His sheep, and this brings comfort to the psalmist.

We need to notice again the order of the psalm's word picture. David is in the midst of crisis. Yet he begins his song about his shepherd God by first portraying God's gracious provision and guidance. Only in this context does he include reflection on God's protection. In his moment of need the psalmist finds comfort in the image of God as his shepherd. But characteristic of his concentration upon God, not himself, is that the psalmist does not first consider God as his problem-solver. God is not merely a "God-of-the-gaps," a God to run to in time of trouble. God is rather his twenty-four-hour-a-day shepherd who provides and leads and, therefore, also protects. God is a God who provides "green pastures." God is a God who leads "in paths of righteousness," and only as such is this same God also with him in life's shadows.

The Lord is my Host. It is not enough for David to portray God as providing, leading and protecting. Both the extent of his crisis and the character of his God demand that he continue his description. Thus the psalmist turns from his word picture of God his Shepherd to describe God as his gracious Host. God not only protects and watches over those whom He is leading, He offers them abundant hospitality.

In Palestine the host was responsible for the well-being of his guests. One recalls, for example, the stories of Abraham's hospitality to the three visitors by the oaks of Mamre (Gen. 18) and of Lot's extreme measures to ensure the safety of his guests in Sodom (Gen. 19). God's provision and blessings are of such a kind. He will not let the threat of attack stop Him from preparing a gracious table. Olive oil will be used to freshen the hair and face of His guests after a long day of travel. A cup so full of refreshment that it literally overflows will be served. God is our lavish supplier. He meets our needs personally and abundantly. Such is the intention of the psalmist's second metaphor.

Again, it is important that the focus of this psalm be kept clear. The psalmist finds hope in time of present crisis by concentrating upon God. He is not concerned with describing his particular plight. (In fact, we never learn the exact nature of his distress.) Neither is he attempting to comment upon his enemies. He would rather have us know his God.

C. S. Lewis, in his *Reflections on the Psalms*, has unfortunately followed Moffatt's (mis)translation of verse 5 and understood God as preparing a feast for David "while my enemies look on." Lewis wonders how the poet's enjoyment can be connected with an open ridiculing of his enemies. Are they to be forced to watch the celebration as God's people gloat? How is this God-honoring? But surely this is misreading the intention of the psalm. We have no reason to gloat, nor should we assume that the enemies are at the banquet table with us. Rather, the psalmist is saying that even in extreme danger God our host provides safety and sustenance. The focus is not on the enemy at all. It is, rather, on God alone who nurtures and protects. He is our host, our comfort, our restorer. We need not want. What a God He is!

Our Life with the Lord

Given the character and nature of his God, given such a good shepherd and gracious host, the psalmist finds his outlook bright. Surely, he says (that is, "without a doubt"), goodness and graciousness will follow him all the days of his life, for God is his God. He is not God's temporary guest. Rather, he will dwell in God's house forever.

Over and over again in the Old Testament God is portrayed as a God of goodness and mercy. "O give thanks to the Lord, for he is good; for his steadfast love endures for ever!" (Ps. 107:1; see also Pss. 118:1,29; 106:1b; 136:1; 1 Chron. 16:34; 2 Chron. 5:13; 7:3; Ezra 3:11). Here is the constant refrain of God's people: "The Lord is good; his steadfast love endures for ever, and his faithfulness to all generations" (Ps. 100:5). Such is the perspective of David in Psalm 23 as well. The two words goodness (*tov*) and mercy (*hesed*) when applied to God are usually associated with the fact that God has covenanted with His people to be their God. To use the imagery of Psalm 23, God has freely contracted to be our Shepherd and Host. God in His steadfast love and goodness has chosen us for His own. Given God's everlasting covenant, the psalmist finds his heart quieted. Is there any doubt that goodness and steadfast love will then follow us all our days if God is a God of goodness and mercy? Not for David!

The phrase "follow me" is somewhat misleading in its English translation for it suggests something more passive than the psalmist intends to communi-

cate. He is not saying goodness and mercy will somehow trail behind or somehow become evident.
Rather, the Hebrew term might be better translated
"pursue." God's goodness and mercy will seek us out.
Here is the psalmist's confidence in time of crisis,
and here is our confidence in time of need. We are not
forced to be the agents of change; God chooses to be.
And thus ongoing goodness and mercy will indeed be
our lot. We can rest confident of the fact. We can also
worship constantly, given that hope.

A New Testament Perspective

David, in time of deep crisis, found in the metaphor of God as a Shepherd a source of confidence and
assurance. In the New Testament, Jesus makes use
of this same imagery, applying it to Himself: "I am the
good shepherd. The good shepherd lays down his life
for the sheep. He who is a hireling and not a shepherd, whose own the sheep are not, sees the wolf
coming and leaves the sheep and flees; and the wolf
snatches them and scatters them. He flees because
he is a hireling and cares nothing for the sheep. I am
the good shepherd; I know my own and my own know
me, as the Father knows me and I know the Father;
and I lay down my life for the sheep. And I have other
sheep, that are not of this fold; I must bring them
also, and they will heed my voice. So there shall be
one flock, one shepherd" (John 10:11-16).

Jesus identifies our salvation not with the fact
that we are special (notice that sheep of other folds
will also be saved), but with His character as a Shepherd. It is of His nature to provide and lead and protect. Here is an explanation of the cross. The cross is
not merely a response to our sin, but the expression
of God's character as Saviour. Jesus states that He

will not permit evil and sin to triumph for He "cares" for the sheep. And He demonstrates that this is indeed the case by dying for us. As Paul expresses it: "God shows his love for us in that while we were yet sinners Christ died for us" (Rom. 5:8).

David was able to find hope in time of present crisis by concentrating on God's character as shepherd and host. And we find these same characteristics of our God being given concrete expression in the person of Jesus Christ, the Son of God. He is our constant Shepherd. We need not worry or fear.

Discussion Questions

1. Would the fact that some shepherds fail to protect their sheep weaken the point of Psalm 23?

2. Doesn't God also want us to express our needs to Him? Should we respond to crises always by praying such a prayer as Psalm 23?

3. We often call poets "inspired" who can paint memorable images in our minds. Is this what makes Psalm 23 inspired?

4. We lead our lives according to basic models or images or stories that we believe to be true to life. How would our lives be shaped if we truly believed God to be our Shepherd and our Host?

5. How are we to understand the phrase "for his name's sake" (v. 3)?

6. What reasons can you give for the psalmist portraying God as protector lastly, after he had spoken of God as providing and leading?

7. Why is Psalm 23 such a favorite psalm?

Note
1. David Hubbard, *Psalms for All Seasons* (Grand Rapids: Eerdmans Publishing Co., 1971), p. 59.

Seven

Psalm 8: God (and Man)

(A Direct Psalm of Praise)

Do we know the difference between praise and thanks? The psalmist's praise focuses on God in and of Himself. The psalmist's thanksgiving responds to how God has acted toward him and his people. The Hymns of Praise tend thus to be of a more general nature, with the specific occasion or event which called forth the praise unrecoverable (see Ps. 149). The Psalms of Thanksgiving, on the other hand, are more specific and often give hints of the background for the songs (see Ps. 116).

The book of Psalms contains a large number of Israel's hymns (Pss. 8; 29; 33; 47; 95-100; 103-105; 111; 113; 114; 117; 145-150). To recognize their nature as praise is crucial to an understanding of them. It is particularly so in the case of Psalm 8. For Psalm 8, unlike the typical hymn of praise, speaks not only of God, but of humankind. It voices wonder not only at God's majesty, but at our own. Without an awareness of the context of praise, without a clear understanding that this description of humankind *follows from* an appreciation of God as God, the reader will misinterpret the psalmist's presentation both of humankind's true glory and of its real limitation.

If we want to praise humanity, let us first, as the writer of Psalm 8 did, praise God. If we are to find value in ourselves (and many of us need desperately to learn how to value ourselves), if we are to judge ourselves worthy we must first come to recognize the infinite worthiness of Almighty God. We must learn how to worship our Lord aright, and then we shall be able to speak confidently concerning ourselves; such is the simple outline the psalmist presents in this hymn.

The order of Psalm 8 (from God to us) is easy to understand intellectually, but difficult, surely, for the modern person to imitate. For we all, even those of us in the Christian community, live in the glow of the "enlightenment." As a society and as individuals we first trust ourselves. It is all too seldom "in God we trust." We marvel at what we can do. We pick what is most impossible (John Kennedy selected "jumping over the moon") and then we make it happen. Some of those who remember the gassings of World War I or the carnage of Auschwitz might question how praiseworthy humankind really is. But memories quickly fade and for the most part we live as though we deserve the praise of others and of ourselves.

Psalm 8 reminds us that it is not our self-sufficiency or honor or ingenuity that is praiseworthy, at least initially. It is, rather, God's name that merits our praise. Here is the psalmist's perspective: "O Lord, our Lord, how majestic is thy name in all the earth!" (vv. 1,9).

Psalm 8: A Hymn of Praise

In the Psalms, the Hymns of Praise are perhaps the simplest in form of any of the songs. What is in the writer's mind is clear to all. In most of the hymns one can discern a general pattern characterized by: (a) a beginning—usually a call to praise; (b) the body—a descriptive statement of the reasons for the praise; and (c) a conclusion—a rounding off of the poem in some manner. This pattern is perhaps most easily observed by looking at Psalms 146-150. Each of these hymns focus on different reasons for praise (God's help, His power, His creation, and so on). However, they all begin and end similarly with the phrase "Praise the Lord."

We can be helped to understand Psalm 8 if we look at each of its parts in turn.

In praise of praise—the beginning (v. 1). The central thrust of the hymn remains its focus on the Godness of God. In order that no doubt remain as to who is to be praised, the psalmist introduces his song with Yahweh's name, with exactly who it is who is majestic. It is the Lord (*Yahweh* in the Hebrew).

It is interesting to note that although Psalm 8 does not use the Hebraic term *hallelujah* (that is, "praise the Lord," *hallelu*—praise, *jah*—short for *Jahweh* or *Yahweh*, "the Lord"), hallelujah opens many of the hymns (see 111:1; 113:1; 117:1; 146:1; 147:1; 148:1; 149:1; 150:1). It is perhaps the original impetus for these Hymns of Praise. It is foundational to Psalm 8. Praise Yahweh! Praise the Lord, for His name is majestic.

The opening verses of the Hymns of Praise often set the mood for all that follows. In Psalm 105, for example, we are called to sing. In Psalm 149 we are told to dance and use lyre and timbrel; in Psalm 29, to dress in holy array. The mood of Psalm 8 is more contemplative. It is not so much an action as an attitude that is sought. The psalmist stands in wonder before the Lord who is also "our Lord" and invites us to join with him. The transcendent, majestic God is also the one who is close at hand, personally involved with us. Truly He should inspire our awe.

Praise is central to the Psalter. The Old Testament scholar Claus Westermann, in his important study of the Psalms makes the point that praise occurs throughout the Psalms, even in the laments of God's people. The Israelite could not approach his God in dialogue without having a word of praise near the tip of his tongue. We have already observed this as we have considered a variety of psalms in the preceding chapters. But though praise is pervasive in the Psalms, one large group of these songs, of which Psalm 8 is representative, focuses exclusively on praise.

Why should we praise God? There are, of course, many reasons which can be offered. Psalm 103:1,2 declares that we should praise God in order not to forget Him.

> Bless the Lord, O my soul;
>> and all that is within me, bless
>> his holy name!
> Bless the Lord, O my soul,
>> and forget not all his benefits.

We praise God in order to make contact with Him. We praise Him in order to affirm that center which integrates our lives and provides meaning for them.

Psalm 8 suggests another reason for praise to God. We praise Him for His name is majestic. That is, we praise Him for He is worthy of our praise. Just as we spontaneously praise whatever we perceive as having value ("What a lovely house"; "What a glorious sunset"; "I just read an absorbing novel"; and so on), so we praise God, the source of all value. Or at least we should! Why is it that for so many it is easy to praise everything from *A* to *Z* of lesser worth and so difficult to praise God? The psalm writer points out the absurdity of such a situation. If other "names" produce praise on our lips—Bach or Mother Theresa or Shakespeare—how much more should the majestic name of our Lord!

The description, Part I (vv. 2-8). The psalm's opening identifies the focus of the hymn for us. God is the subject, a God who is at one and the same time majestic ("O Lord") and personal ("our Lord"). This dual orientation, seemingly a paradox, accounts for much of the force of the psalm. God is both eminent and immanent, regal and fatherly. What is God like? God is all powerful. His glory is chanted above the heavens. He stills the enemy and the avenger. The heavens are His work; we are reminded of Genesis 1. Yet this transcendent God shows Himself also to be loving and caring. Even babes and infants know Him and sing His glory. *Yahweh* ("the Lord") not only established the stars, He crowned humanity with glory and honor. God's personal involvement and concern for humankind recalls Genesis 2.

It is crucial that such a juxtaposition of God's otherness from us and His personal involvement with us be held onto in our day as well. The Judeo-Christian God is not simply a domesticated grandfather or an all-powerful dictator. He is neither solely majestic nor solely caring. He is both. This basic fact of the Godhead is so easily lost sight of. We tend as a society to hold to one of two extremes. Either we picture God as

one with us—forgiving, loving, not expecting too
much—with the result that we either are soon ele-
vated to God's status or God is trivialized and
brought down to our level. Or, conversely, we picture
God as removed from us—majestic, mysterious,
someone to be feared—with the result that His personal relationship with us is forgotten. The psalmist's hymn of praise rejects such one-sidedness with
its resultant distortions. Instead the hymn revels in
the paradox of God's being, emphasizing both His
tender lovingkindness and His all-powerful sovereignty.

Such a portrayal of the extremes of God's per-
sonhood is consistent with the broader biblical message, too. Recall how the Lord's Prayer begins, "Our
Father who art in *heaven.*" Here is the same dual
focus. God is our Father (Jesus, on another occasion,
even called God *Abba,* "Daddy," Mark 14:36). He is
also in heaven, regal and transcendent. A review of
Jesus' personal prayers confirms this same dual orientation. In Matthew 11:25 it is recorded that Jesus
prayed, "I thank thee, Father, Lord of heaven and
earth . . . " God is both Lord and Father. We must neither distance nor domesticate Him. God reveals His
true character as fully embodying both extremes.

The description, Part II (vv. 5-8). Having focused
upon the majesty of his God, the psalmist is
reminded of his own insignificance (v. 4). The pattern is a familiar one in Scripture. Consider Isaiah as
he is called to be a prophet (Isa. 6) or Moses as he
stands before the burning bush (Exod. 3): to come
into God's presence is to sense our unworthiness.
Similarly, to truly praise God is to be reminded that
praise is due to Him alone.

But here the psalmist injects a surprising twist

into this Hymn of Praise. Rather than turning to a confession of sin (something that would be appropriate if one were looking primarily at oneself, and at God only as He is in relation to us) the psalmist turns to a description of God's finest creation.

This can be appropriate only if one is looking first of all at God and only afterward at man/woman as he/she reflects God's glory. Despite the human logic of our being insignificant, the hymn writer finds that from God's perspective we are significant—in fact, "little less than God." As creatures of God we are filled with honor. Rather than focus on human misery, the psalmist boldly declares our glory as creations of God.

The psalmist sings of the greatness of men and women. However, even the grammar of his words suggests that this human praise flows from his understanding of God. God is the subject of each of the psalmist's sentences; humankind is the object, the predicate. Thus the psalmist writes, " . . . thou has made him . . . dost crown him . . . thou hast given him . . . thou hast put all things under his feet . . . " (vv. 5,6). God is the one who is glorious. Ours is but a reflected glory.

Even if it is reflected (or better, because it is reflected), humankind's glory is genuine. Such a message needs to be heard in our day and age when a good self-image seems so hard to achieve. We know countless folk who seem unable to accept themselves. Contemporary writers from Beckett to Updike try desperately to find some meaning in life for men and women. Psychiatrists' offices are filled with people who can't accept themselves. We work with many who suffer from either a sense of unimportance or a feeling of over-importance.

What has gone wrong? The psalm suggests one

fundamental answer: as a society, our focus upon humankind is largely independent of God, and therefore largely independent of men and women as God's finest creation. On the day of President Reagan's inauguration, for example, we as a country ritually thanked God for rescuing the hostages from Iran. But such activities were largely window dressing. They are not taken seriously by many. Nor do they affect the situation significantly. When God is considered chiefly as an ornament or a problem-solver, is it any wonder that we cannot better accept ourselves? Exhibiting in our daily lives a practical denial of our creaturehood we are perplexed by resulting anxieties. We should not be.

Psalm 8 provides an alternate perspective toward ourselves—a God-given perspective. We need neither to whitewash our failure and sin nor to grovel in it. Instead we can proclaim ourselves glorious, for God does. The perspective of the psalm writer is that of Genesis 1 and 2, of Adam and Eve before the Fall. God honors the apex of His creation by giving them, both male and female (Gen. 1:26,27), dominion over the earth. But note that the focus remains always on the Creator, not on even the finest of His creation. Given God's majesty, it is ludicrous to speak of human glory independent of His creative choice.

The conclusion (v. 9) Given the incredible fact of human glory, is it any wonder that the psalmist returns to his opening refrain to complete the psalm? Certainly only a majestic God could create something as wonderful as humankind. When one considers all that humanity has the ability to achieve, when humankind's dominion over all the earth is examined, it becomes even clearer how majestic our Creator is. "O Lord, our Lord, how majestic is thy name in all the earth!'"

Conclusion

The writer of Hebrews adds an important commentary on Psalm 8 in the second chapter of his book. In quoting from verses 4 through 6 of the psalm, the writer applies the praise of man specifically to Jesus. Just as Psalm 8 finds its inspiration in Adam and Eve (in Gen. 1 and 2), so the Christina discovers the psalm's full embodiment in the Second Adam (Heb. 2). At creation man received his glory and honor as he (and she) was created in the image of God, created, that is, for loving relationship with Him. But humankind fell. We sinned, and we continue to sin. For this reason our intended glory (our ability to love God and neighbor) has become our misery and our death.

The writer of Hebrews therefore reminds us that it is only in Jesus—only in the Son of Man, in that one who was "crowned with glory and honor because of the suffering of death" (v. 9)—that we now can see the true glory of humankind. Our original glory in creation is reaffirmed in Jesus Christ's re-creation of us. Our majestic Lord, the great God of the universe, showed Himself to be our Saviour, or Re-creator. By His action, our glory can once again be manifested. We no longer need fear being overcome by temptation and death (Heb. 2:14-18).

Having affirmed Jesus as Lord we can recognize our self-worth, for God has. Having confessed our faith in Jesus Christ we can understand who we are in God's sight. We are worthwhile to the Creator of the universe, who is our Redeemer. If we praise God in Christ we can also rejoice in who we are, for God does. Hallelujah!

Discussion Questions

1. In what way can Psalm 8 be viewed as a commentary on Genesis 1 and 2?

2. In which verses do you find a dual focus upon God's majesty and His grace?

3. In what ways does the psalmist express his desire to dwell primarily on God rather than man?

4. In what other books of the Old Testament do we find the creative tension between God's eminence and His immanence, His holiness and His love emphasized?

5. Read Philippians 4:8,9. How does Psalm 8 shed light on this admonition of Paul?

6. What is the difference between praise and thanksgiving?

Eight

Psalm 19: God's Signatures upon Life

(An Indirect Hymn of Praise)

"I take this [Ps. 19] to be the greatest poem in the Psalter and one of the greatest lyrics in the world," C. S. Lewis.

"Earth's crammed with heaven, and every common bush aflame with God; but only those who see take off their shoes, the rest sit round it and pluck blackberries," Elizabeth Barrett Browning.

There are two general ways of praising another: *directly*, by focusing on that individual, or *indirectly*, by exulting in something or someone closely associated with that person—a child, an accomplishment, and so on. For example, one might comment upon what fine taste a particular friend has. On the other hand one might mention the beautiful dress she is wearing. Again one might remark about a person's intelligence, or he might praise the book she has written.

This is also true of our praise of God. The Israelites praised God *directly* for who He was (as we have seen in Psalm 8). They also praised Him in hymns, by singing of that which was identified with Him—Zion, the city of God; the Temple, the house of God; the Law, the Word of God; Creation, an act of God. Psalm 19 is a Hymn of Praise to God which makes use of an indirect approach. God is praised but through reflection upon His creation and by reference to His Law.

Psalm 19: A Hymn of Praise

We observed in chapter 7 that hymns in the Psalter tend to follow the general form: introduction, body, and then conclusion. But there is also much variety in the application of this general pattern. Often the introductory call to praise is the word *hallelujah* ("praise the Lord"); but as we observed in our study of Psalm 8, this basic form is by no means mandatory for the psalm writer. In Psalm 19, for instance, the psalmist, in his eagerness to identify his reasons for praise, does in fact do away with the introductory call to praise and instead leaps right into his explanation. We are to praise the Lord because the heavens are telling of His glory.

The psalmist's praise of his God is divided into three quite distinct sections in Psalm 19. This has led some to suggest that the song is actually a combination of two different hymns—the psalmist using an earlier psalm on creation and combining it with his reflections on the Law and on his own sin. This is possible, but by no means necessary, as I shall suggest. The praise of God as seen in His general revelation in creation (vv. 1-6) calls forth praise of God as seen in His specific revelation in His Law, that is, in Scripture (vv. 7-11). This in turn calls forth recognition of the psalmist's unworthiness and his need to be kept from sin (vv. 12, 13).

The psalm ends with a distinctive petition (v. 14),

a closing suggested by the psalmist's reflection on his own situation. Verse 14 is a humble request to God to accept the writer's words of praise. As we again note the variation from the typical closing of a hymn ("praise the Lord"), we are reminded that the psalmists are not merely technicians cranking out poetry according to stock forms. They are "inspired" writers in both the popular and the theological senses of that word.

"God" in the Psalm

We can best begin to understand this psalm by looking at its description of God. In the first half of the psalm the general name for divinity is used, "God" (Hebrew, *El*). This is the common title for the Father of the Gods used by the ancient Semitic peoples (*El Shaddai*, God Almighty, Gen. 17:1; *El 'Olam*, the Everlasting God, Gen. 21:33; *El Bethel*, the God of Bethel, Gen. 31:13; *Ishmael*, God hears, Gen. 16:11).

In the second half of the psalm the special, revered name for Israel's divinity is used, "The Lord" (Hebrew, *Yahweh*). Thus in the names used for God Himself we find suggested that progression from general to special revelation which is basic to the structure of the psalm. All humanity can hear God's glory if they will but listen to creation (see Rom. 1:19,20, where Paul shifts the imagery from sound to sight, describing God's revelation of Himself not as soundless voice or wordless speech but as invisible presence). However, it is in the Law of the Lord that God's word is perfectly heard.

There is perhaps a third reference to divinity in this psalm. The writer uses in his description of nature's glory some of the images found in the pagan story of a god of the sun whose abode at night was in the "sea" where he rested in the arms of his beloved, only to arise at dawn, refreshed and having full vigor and radiance for his dash across the skies. But notice what the psalmist does to this myth. He defuses it. He renders it harmless by reinterpreting it in the light of his faith in God as the Creator of nature and its Revealer. There is no deified sun or moon, only the Creator whose glory is revealed in and through His creation, the sun. The psalmist is aware of the misconceptions of God which exist in the larger culture about him and he desires to challenge these false religious beliefs of his neighbors.

The "Speech" of God in Creation (vv. 1-6)

Jim Houston, in his book *I Believe in the Creator*, points out that in Psalm 19 "there is mystery in the utterance of Creation." There is "speech . . . [yet] there is no speech"; the night "declares knowledge" but its "voice is not heard" (vv. 2,3). Houston comments, "God the Creator is recognizable in all the handiwork of the universe, but not describable in human terms; it is not saving knowledge for man."

In his story "Packed Dirt, Churchgoing, A Dying Cat, A Traded Car" the novelist John Updike portrays a similar understanding of God's revelation. God's voice is heard through nature, although in a way that lacks sufficient clarity. The story focuses upon David Kern who is reminiscing about four events in his life that spoke to him of larger patterns of meaning not of his own devising. One of the vignettes concerns a dying cat which David discovered on the highway at the same time his wife lay in labor at the hospital. He stopped and cared for the cat, even writing a note to its owners in the event they later found their cat dead. But as he huddled over the animal David later related, "It suggested I was making too much fuss, and seemed to say to me, *Run on home.*" Later that night the phone rang telling David of the birth of his daughter. Human life had, at that moment, an increased significance. David described this event of cat-plus-baby-daughter as "supernatural mail." He said it "had the signature: decisive but illegible." As with the psalmist, Updike writes of a speech that is not literally speech, not audible, however strongly it is heard.

God's aesthetic signatures are everywhere over His landscape. One need only wonder at a sunrise or become lost in awe at the stars as the psalmist has. One need only marvel at the birth of a child as David Kern did. If we will open ourselves up to God's creation we will find the Creator there; God will in His grace speak to us. One need not even go beyond oneself as God's creature in order to sense something of God's presence. The story is told that after Helen Keller's teacher, Anne Sullivan, had given her the names of physical objects in sign language, Miss Sullivan attempted to explain God and tapped out the symbols for the name "God." Much to Miss Sullivan's surprise, Helen spelled back, "Thank you for telling me God's name, Teacher, for he has touched me many times before." Helen Keller, like David Fern and like our psalmist, knew something of God's signature from nature, but it was wordless. It was not yet "perfect." It lacked sufficient definition. There was need of further revelation.

A Second Form of Speech (vv. 7-10)

C. S. Lewis, in his otherwise helpful analysis of Psalm 19, argues that the actual words of the psalm supply no logical connection between its first (vv. 1-6) and second (vv. 7-11) movements. How could the psalmist move from a reflection on creation to forthright praise of the Law? The answer comes in part as we note the variety of words concerning our "speech" which is found in verses 1 through 4: "telling . . . proclaims . . . pours forth speech . . . declares . . . speech . . . words . . . voice . . . voice and words. . . ." Here is the trigger for the psalmist's reflection on the Word of God. Having portrayed creation in the form of a "word," the psalmist turns to consider the Word of God, the Law. It is this further and clarifying speech of God—His "law . . . testimony . . . precepts . . . commandment . . . ordinances"—that engages the psalmist's thought.

The Word of God is praised, for though the speech of creation is poured forth, it is not heard. It is silent speech. It is everywhere present yet it also needs further clarification, given our sin (vv. 11-13). It is only God's special revelation, exemplified by the Law, which fully illumines. To the Law can be added the Prophets and Writings as well—that is, the remainder of the Old Testament—for such is consistent with the psalmist's intent. God's revelation, moreover, culminates in Jesus, the Word incarnate. And the New Testament provides the inspired record and interpretation of the Christ event. Together the Word incarnate and the Word written prove to be "perfect," "sure," "right," "pure," "clean," and "true." Here is the psalmist's perspective as he offers praise for the Law.

C. S. Lewis speaks of initially finding the psalmist's delight in the Law "utterly bewildering." He says, " 'Thou shalt not steal, Thou shalt not commit adultery'—I can understand that a man can, and must, respect these 'statutes,' and try to obey them and assent to them in his heart. But it is very hard to find how they could be, so to speak, delicious, how they exhilarate." How can the psalmists revel in the Law as the writer of Psalm 1 does? How can he say that "his delight is in the law of the Lord, and on his law he meditates day and night" (Ps. 1:2)?

Perhaps the finest example of taking delight in the Law is Psalm 119, the longest psalm in the collection and one of the most carefully crafted and elaborate. The psalm is divided into sections, or stanzas, each beginning with successive letters of the Hebrew alphabet. Each section has eight verses which provide a variation on a series of words which are more or less synonyms (law, testimonies, precepts, statutes, commandments, ordinances, word). The poem obviously is not a sudden creation. Lewis says, "It is a pattern, a thing done like embroidery, stitch by stitch, through long, quiet hours, for love of subject and for the delight in leisurely, disciplined craftsmanship." It is the Law which triggers this devotion. How can this be?

Psalm 19 provides a clear answer. In this hymn the Law is described as "perfect." It is that which "revives the soul" and makes "wise the simple," that causes rejoicing of the heart and an enlightenment of one's eyes. Is it any wonder that the Law is more desirable than gold and sweeter than honey? Not at all. For the Law is portrayed here not primarily as a *burden* or obstacle (though something of this obverse side appears in verses 11 through 13), but as a *blessing*.

The Law is first of all a manifestation of God's grace. The Law is His means of clarifying the speech of creation, of amplifying its words so that now God's voice does contain "speech" and His words have sound (see v. 3). Psalm 119 expresses this desire for greater clarity well: "Deal bountifully with thy servant, that I may live and observe thy word. Open my eyes, that I may behold wondrous things out of thy law. I am a sojourner on earth; hide not thy commandments from me!" (Ps. 119:17-19)

There is no hint in such psalms as Psalms 19 and 119 of the Law as a burden, a judgment that came to be expressed in Paul's day. There is no need here to distinguish between "Law" and "spirit" as Paul does in trying to clarify the nature of grace (see 2 Cor. 3:6). Rather, with the Apostle John, the psalmist affirms that God's "commandments are not burdensome" (1 John 5:3).

The description the psalmist offers of the Law is worthy of further comment. Perhaps the reference to the sun in verses 5 and 6 helps focus his comments on the Law. Like the sun the Law of the Lord is "perfect." It is, in the words of Samuel Terrien, "sound, round, and complete, for it restores life to the inward man." God's testimony is also "sure," that is, reliable. It cannot be ignored and is, like the sun, capable of breaking through to the most simple person. The Lord's precepts are "right." That is, there is nothing crooked about them. They thrust their shafts of light like arrows winging to a target.

Like the sun, the Law ("commandment") is "pure," or bright. The same word in the Hebrew, *bārāh* ("pure"), is used in the Song of Solomon to describe the sun's rays directly ("bright as the sun," Song of Sol. 6:10). Like the sun, the Law enlightens the eyes, causing a person to move ahead in full awareness of his goal. "The fear of the Lord," which in this context means obedience to the divine commands, is also "clean." Lacking impurity it will

endure like the sun (see Ps. 72:5, "May he live while
the sun endures"). Finally, the Law ("ordinances") is
"true" and "righteous." It divides right from wrong,
good from evil. The writer to the Hebrews expressed a
similar idea using as the basic metaphor not the sun
but a sword: "For the word of God is living and active,
sharper than any two-edged sword, piercing to the
division of soul and spirit, of joints and marrow, and
discerning the thoughts and intentions of the heart"
(Heb. 4:12). Like the sun itself, the light from God's
Word is desirable. It is more precious, says the psalmist, than fine gold and sweeter than honey.

God (and Man) Revisited (vv. 11-14)

In chapter 7 we observed that within the context
of his praise for *God*, the writer of Psalm 8 found reason to praise humanity as well. From God the psalmist turned to focus upon "man." This is an important
truth based in the message of Genesis 1 and 2. We
are created in the image of God and have been given
dominion over all the earth. But Genesis 3 follows
Genesis 1 and 2. And as we know, the Fall affects our
glory. It is this alternate side of the creation account
that is emphasized in Psalm 19. To encounter God in
His full revelation is to become aware of our fundamental unworthiness. Thus the psalmist moves from
praise to petition (something as uncharacteristic of
the Hymns of Praise as is Psalm 8's praise of humankind). He cries out, "Keep back thy servant also from
presumptuous sins."

In an age which can be characterized by humankind's hubris, by a false sense of pride and a non-
authentic independence, we need to reflect on Psalm
19. Without the grace of God we will err. We will sin.
The psalmist realizes that even his very words of

praise might in some way be presumptuous and self-serving. Who can be sure of his motives? Who can sort out the complete ramifications of his action? Thus, it is on a cautious, humble note that the psalmist ends his Hymn of Praise.

There is no arrogance here. It is not the hymn writer's opinion and action that are praiseworthy. Rather, it is God alone, God who is his rock and redeemer. Having experienced God's revelation in creation and re-creation (the Law), the psalmist is overcome with joy. In his need to express this joy, he sings praise to his God. Yet he also feels inadequate in doing so. Thus he asks God to accept his incomplete expression, trusting Him that He will certainly do so.

Discussion Questions

1. Many of the gospel hymns we sing use tunes that were once secular drinking songs. Here (vv. 5,6) is another example of faithfully transforming what was pagan. What advantage or disadvantage is there in using sacredly that which is secular?

2. What is the relationship between creation and the Law as reflected in this psalm?

3. In what way can verses 7-13 be seen as a qualifier upon verses 1-6 to protect the listener from faulty conclusions concerning God's revelation in nature?

4. Can a person know God by allowing the "heavens to tell the glory of God"?

5. Besides the brilliance of a sunrise and the splendor of a starry night, what other aspects of creation have declared God's glory to *you*?

6. Compare the responses of Isaiah at the Temple (Isa. 6) and of Moses before the burning bush (Exod. 3) with the psalmist's response here. In what ways

are these responses to God's revelation similar and in what ways different?

Nine

Psalm 30: Giving Thanks Biblically

(A Song of Individual Thanksgiving)

As Moses came to the end of his life, the book of Deuteronomy records, he addressed his people, seeking to prepare them for their new life with God in the land which they had been promised. He concluded his lengthy address by challenging God's people with these words: "See, I have set before you this day life and good, death and evil. If you obey the commandments of the Lord your God . . . then you shall live. . . . But if your heart turns away . . . you shall perish;. . . I have set before you life and death, blessing and curse; therefore, choose life . . . loving the Lord your God, obeying his voice, and cleaving to him" (Deut. 30:15-20).

Throughout the Old Testament this challenge to "choose life" is voiced again and again. We are, for example, to be wise, "For he who finds me [wisdom] finds life and obtains favor from the Lord; but he who misses me injures himself; all who hate me love death" (Prov. 8:35,36).

In the Old Testament life is celebrated as a gift

from the Lord. Longevity of days is not in itself valuable, but is precious only because it is the occasion for our ongoing relationship with God. Life is valuable for it is here that we encounter our Lord. Life is to be prized, for life itself is evidence of God's favor.

Psalm 30 is a Psalm of Individual Thanksgiving, a song of praise to God for His deliverance from the threat of death. It is a psalm that "chooses life"—life from God and for God. The psalmist had forgotten that all he had was from God. He had forgotten to fear the Lord and had encountered God's anger. But in his sickness he has turned to God, his gracious helper. And God has met him. With thankful heart the psalmist recommends to all God's "saints" that they sing praises to the Lord.

Psalm 30: A Psalm of Individual Thanksgiving

In discussing the Psalm of Trust in chapter 6, of which Psalm 23 is the best known, we observed that they have a very close relationship with the Psalms of Lament (chapters 2 and 3). In fact, the Psalm of Trust is simply an expanded form of the statement of trust typically present in most of the laments. Similarly, we can also find in the lament the "origin" of the Psalm of Thanksgiving. For the song of thanksgiving is also an expanded form of the vow of thanksgiving found in many of the laments. Psalm 57, for example, concludes its lament with these words:

> I will give thanks to thee, O Lord,
>   among the peoples;
> I will sing praises to thee among
>   the nations.
> For thy steadfast love is great
>   to the heavens,
>   thy faithfulness to the clouds.

Be exalted, O God, above the heavens!
Let thy glory be over all the
earth! (Ps. 57:9-11).

There is in the Psalm of Lament a movement from
complaint (Ps. 13) or penitence (Ps. 51) to thanksgiving and praise. Certain that God will intervene, and
in anticipation of God's response to his cry, the
psalmist ends his lament with a vow to praise God
(see also Ps. 13:6; 51:14,15). It is these "vows to
praise God" that become the bases for the Psalms of
Thanksgiving (see Pss. 30; 32; 34; 66; 92; 116; 138).
However, rather than being offered *in anticipation* of
God's deliverance, they are now the grateful songs of
God's people *in response* to His saving grace.

The typical form of these psalms is quite simple,
again like the Psalms of Trust. Psalm 30 can be out-
lined as follows: (1) An opening address praising God
(30:1a); (2) A summary of why the thanksgiving is
called for (30:1b-3); (3) A narration of the psalmist's
plight, petition, rescue, and praise (30:6-12a); (4) A
concluding expression of praise (30:12b).

In Psalm 30 this basic outline is enriched by a call
to the surrounding listeners asking them to join the
psalmist in praise (vv. 4,5). If verses 1 through 5 are
viewed as an extended exclamation of thankful
praise, we can understand the psalm as being the
narration of the psalmist's experience, flanked by two
statements of praise.

*The opening address: proclaiming God's praise
(v. 1a).* Psalm 30 concerns God, not man. The
psalmist makes this crystal clear as he begins his
psalm: "I will extol thee, O Lord . . ." By relating how
God has intervened in time of need, by describing
how God has worked in his own life, the songwriter

attempts both to thank his Lord and to deepen the understanding of the Lord's people concerning their God.

Psalm 30 is a song of thanksgiving. It relates how God has answered the prayer of a single faithful person, restoring him to health. But it is far different than most songs of thanks we might compose, for our expression of gratitude is too often preoccupied with ourselves. The one being thanked sometimes gets slight mention. We are so happy to have our situation changed or a favor granted that we focus almost exclusively on what has happened to *us*. Not so with the psalmist. His focus is on God. To emphasize this fact, the Old Testament scholar Claus Westermann labels such Psalms of Thanksgiving, "Psalms of Narrative Praise" (as distinct from the Hymns of Praise). He points out that our word "thank" has no corresponding word in the Hebrew language, the language of the psalm writers. What is often translated as "thank" in our English Bibles really means praise to God for a specific act which has just taken place. Even in describing his crisis and God's answer, the psalmist centers on praising God.

An introductory summary (vv. 1b-3). In most of the Psalms of Individual Thanksgiving the introductory summary is a single sentence. But in the case of Psalm 30 the psalmist is so overcome with what God has done in his life that he feels compelled to anticipate all that his psalm will declare. It is not sufficient merely to say that God lifted him up (for example, rescued him from the pit of death, see v. 3). No, God has not only rescued him, He has silenced the psalmist's enemies, responding to the author's cry by healing him, indeed bringing him back from the edge of death and restoring him to life.

The religious beliefs of Israel's neighbors centered in a cyclical view of life. The Baal religion, which characterized Canaanite faith, found hope in the cycle of the seasons that moved through the bleakness of winter into the renewal of life in the spring. The meaning of life was thus tied to the rhythms of nature (hence the saying, "hope springs eternal"). How different was the shape of Israel's faith. God's actions were not seen as being restricted to recurring cycles. Rather God was a God of history who acted decisively within it, altering its course according to His will and purposes. The Israelites' God was the God of the Exodus, a God who responded to the cry of His people and thus intervened in history. It is this historical God to whom Psalm 30 witnesses: "O Lord, my God, I cried to thee for help, and thou hast healed me" (v. 2).

Psalm 30 recounts God's deliverance of the psalmist from death. He has figuratively, if not quite literally, been in "Sheol," in the "Pit," that place of the dead where Israel believed people retained only the faintest resemblance of life. A. A. Anderson is perhaps correct in describing how Sheol functions in this psalm, "not so much [as] a geographical location as a sphere of influence: wherever one finds the characteristics of Sheol, such as weakness, disease, misery, forsakenness, etc., there is Sheol also."

The author of Psalm 88 poetically describes a similar situation:

> I am reckoned among those who go down
> to the Pit;
> I am a man who has no strength,
> like one forsaken among the dead,
> like the slain that lie in the grave,
> like those whom thou dost remember no

more,
for they are cut off from thy hand.
Thou hast put me in the depths of the
Pit,
in the regions dark and deep (Ps. 88:4-
6; see also Ps. 18:4,5).

The psalmist senses the futility of his life outside of
God's presence. Here is the horror of death for the
Israelite: God is thought to be absent (v. 7; Ps. 139:8
is an interesting exception to this general understanding of Sheol in the Old Testament, although its
poetic language should not be over-interpreted).

In Sheol there is no praise of Yahweh, no recounting of His faithfulness and steadfast love. In his song
of thanksgiving which is recorded in Isaiah, Hezekiah expresses this fear of death, saying:
For Sheol cannot thank thee;
death cannot praise thee;
those who go down to the pit cannot hope
for thy faithfulness.
The living, the living, he thanks thee,
as I do this day;
the father makes known to the children
thy faithfulness (Isa. 38:18,19).

This is the perspective also of the writer of Psalm
30. He cries out to his Lord, "Will the dust praise
thee?" (v. 9). The real horror of his illness is not its
pain or discomfort. Neither is his desire for physical
health merely the hope of added years of life. Longevity is no blessing in itself. Rather, life is desired by
the psalmist, for only then is one's relationship with
God secure and his praises possible.

Israel's faith is characterized by what Bernhard

Anderson has called "a robust this-worldliness." This life is not viewed as a mere preparation for the next. No, present life is to be enjoyed for what it is; it is for "dancing" unto the Lord and for "gladness." Though sickness may come; though one might even experience a seeming "God-forsakenness," the psalmists pray that these moments may be transformed into occasions of thanksgiving and praise. And they are. The Israelites believe they must "see the goodness of the Lord in the land of the living" (Ps. 27:13). They cry for rescue here and now. And God meets them in their need, bringing them life. Can we not learn an important lesson from the Old Testament concerning the value and joy of present life with our Lord?

The imagery of rescue used in Psalm 30 is particularly expressive. The Lord has "drawn up" (30:1) the psalmist from the Pit of death, much as a person would draw up a bucket from a well. (In fact, the same verb is used in just that sense in Exod. 2:16 and its noun form means "bucket" in Isa. 40:15.) From terrible depths that afforded no escape, God has rescued the songwriter, restoring him to light. One can almost feel the joy of the psalmist as he grabs hold of the rope which pulls him to safety. From the fear of the night, God has ushered him into the joy of the morning. Truly, thanksgiving is warranted.

An expression of praise (vv. 4,5). The Hebrew word *hōdah* ("to give thanks," v. 4) sometimes has the wider meaning of "to acknowledge or confess or proclaim." The psalmist wants to sing praises to God, "to proclaim" His holy name. This praise is not praise of God in general terms, as in the Hymns of Praise. (In chap. 7 we considered Psalm 8 where God is extolled for who He is: the Creator of all, the giver of the Law, and so on.) Instead, the psalmist's praise of

God is now focused specifically in response to God's direct intervention on behalf of the writer.[1]

Verses 4 and 5 contain a call to the author's fellow-worshipers to join him in praise of God. The psalmist turns to the "saints" (the *hasidim*, the covenant-people; the same word is used to describe faithful, ultra-orthodox Jews today) and asks them to join in this hymn. Having summarized the intention of his psalm—to praise God for his rescue—the writer realizes that his experience is but a single example of a wider pattern. The God who has mercifully met his need is the gracious God who meets all needs. The God who has turned his mourning and weeping into joy and dancing is one who can be characterized by the joy He brings to all His people. Thus, before recounting his particular experience in more detail, the psalmist calls his worshiping listeners to praise God, for it is the Lord's nature to grant favors and bring joy: "His anger is but for a moment, and his favor is for a lifetime" (v. 5a; see also Isa. 54:7-10). The psalmist's experience is viewed as a microcosm of wider reality. His experience is important not simply for itself but because it is a witness to the "name" (v. 4; that is, to the very nature) of God. His experience validates his sharing the good news.

Psalm 30 is a reminder to all who have experienced God's grace that good news is to be shared. In praise, in thanksgiving, in worship, we are to testify to our Lord's saving deeds. The psalmist offered his individual perspective and through it the entire worshiping community found blessing. We know this is the case, for the psalm's title, "A Song at the Dedication of the Temple," reveals that the psalm eventually had deep significance for God's people as a whole. Although added at a later date than its original composition (the titles are not part of the inspired writing), this title reveals that in Psalm 30 God's people found expression of a fundamental pattern of experience. And so the psalm was used in the praise of God at the Temple dedication service. It is still used by Jews today during Hanukkah, when the rededication of the Temple is recalled.

A narration of the psalmist's experience (vv. 6-12a). Psalm 30 relates the typical situation found in Psalms of Thanksgiving. Although he was once prosperous, the psalmist was brought low (vv. 6,7). He cried to the Lord asking for help so that he could again praise God (vv. 8-10). And God did indeed respond, turning his mourning into dancing (vv. 11,12a).

We do not know the exact situation that lay behind this psalm, but the crisis involved some serious illness (v. 2). The psalmist had seemed "a strong mountain," secure, carefree, and prosperous. There is a hint of pride involved in the assertion. He was wrongly self-sufficient and complacent. Only in retrospect does he realize that his strength was in reality a blessing from God, that his prosperity depended solely on God's goodness. Thus, when God chose to "hide his face," the psalmist was stricken with illness and seemed close to death. In his anguish, the writer uttered a Psalm of Lament, pleading with God that since he now recognized God's Lordship, his death would serve no purpose. He asked for health so that he might again tell of God's faithfulness. (Here is the typical pattern for a Lament; see chap. 2.) And God answered him, giving him every reason to fulfill his vow to praise the Lord. It is for this reason, the fulfillment of his pledge, that the psalmist enters God's house of worship and extols his Lord.

Although the historical circumstances of the song's composition are not described in Israel's songbook (the Psalms), in other portions of the Old Testament the settings of such psalms are explicitly given. These can be instructive for us. In Isaiah 38 it is recounted that King Hezekiah was sick and at the point of death (v. 1). He prayed, voicing a lament, protesting his innocence and asserting his continuing faith (v. 3). Then after Isaiah spoke a message of assurance to him and he was healed by the Lord, Hezekiah composed a Psalm of Thanksgiving to God (vv. 10-20).

The book of Jonah provides a second illustration. In its second chapter there is an account of how Jonah cried out to the Lord in distress after the great fish had swallowed him up. He vowed to praise God if he were delivered, and Jonah was faithful to that vow. Sensing God's deliverance at work even before he was disgorged, Jonah saying a Psalm of Thanksgiving to the Lord (Jon. 2:2-9), a song that Israel later used as its thanksgiving as well.

In each case the reversal of the psalmist's suffering is understood as being the activity of God Himself. Here is not the removed God of the philosophers, a first-cause who is now aloof from His creation. Instead, Scripture presents God as personal and responsive. In Genesis 3 He clothes the man and the woman as a sign of forgiveness. In Exodus He reveals His name to Moses. In Judges He dampens Gideon's fleece. For David He guides that rock which fells Goliath. God's saints, His children, truly have something to sing praises about: the eternal God is present and responsive, turning mourning into dancing.

A concluding expression of praise (v. 12b). Psalm 30 ends with a promise that this praise of God will be ongoing. Claus Westermann states the psalmist's intention well: "It is not as if the Psalmist had completed a 'thank you' to God, as we might express it; the narrative praise streams out into the expanse of existence which henceforth is to be marked by praise." Our thanks both to others and to God is too often a "throw-away" phrase, a quickly forgotten tagline. It fails to become, as it should, a total way of living. The person who has truly experienced God's grace at one point in time has seen enough to be able to praise God at all points in life. We need not wait for special occasions. God can and should be praised as a general style of life, for His name *is* praiseworthy.

This psalm ends with a vow to offer ongoing hymns of praise to the Lord. The psalmist, a single individual who experienced God's saving grace in one particular instance, is moved to offer ongoing description concerning God's grace. Psalms 8 and 19, which we have already studied, are two examples of this more general praise. Our thanks should expand into ongoing praise. Our focus on *what God has done* should remind us of *who God is*.

Conclusion

These Psalms of Thanksgiving which are found in the Psalter eventually became detached from their original setting and were sung instead as spiritual songs in early Judaic worship. We have noted that the title of Psalm 30 gives us one indication of this fact. Although the song was originally composed by someone who had been restored from a serious illness, it came to be used as a Communal Song of Thanksgiving to the Lord who had restored His people's fortunes. Such a universalizing process for these individual thanksgiving songs is, of course, the psalm writer's intention. For he exhorts: "Sing praises to the Lord, O you his saints, and give thanks to his holy name" (v. 4).

The Individual Psalms of Thanksgiving found in the Psalter thus became the general songs of praise of the people of God. And as such they entered as well into the worship of the early Christian community. Here is the context of Paul's admonition to the Ephesians: "Be filled with the Spirit, addressing one another in psalms and hymns and spiritual songs, singing and making melody to the Lord with all your heart, always and for everything giving thanks in the name of our Lord Jesus Christ to God the Father" (Eph. 5:18b-20).

We are to focus on the giver, not the gift; on God's graciousness and not on our sufficiency. Forgetting this, we become like the psalmist in his short-lived prosperity, like the rich man whom Jesus described as foolish in his mistaken sense of ease (Luke 12:16-21). We need to continually be glad before the Lord, recognizing that it is "in him we live and move and have our being" (Acts 17:28).

Discussion Questions

1. In what way are the Psalms of Lament (such as Ps. 13) and the Psalms of Thanksgiving (such as Ps. 30) related?

2. In what way are the Psalms of Thanksgiving and the Hymns of Praise (such as Ps. 19) related?

3. Why, primarily, is death lamented by the psalmist? What new insight does Christ provide?

4. Throughout the Old Testament we are challenged to choose life. What is life, according to the psalmist?

5. Read the story of King Hezekiah in Isaiah 38:1-

20. What similarities do you find with Psalm 30? Does it suggest one possible scenario for Psalm 30?

6. Jonah 2:2-9 contains another Psalm of Thanksgiving. Can you find similarities in its shape and outline with Psalm 30? What is surprising about its location in chapter 2?

7. What place should individual testimony have in the life of the believer? Read 1 Timothy 1:12-17.

Note

1. Some psalms are a blend of the Hymn of Praise and the Song of Thanksgiving. There seems to be a specific act of God's mercy that has inspired them, yet their focus is on God and who He is, not on the God who has answered prayers (see Ps. 100, which is a Hymn of Praise but is labeled "A Psalm for the thank offering"). Although the Psalms of Thanks and Praise thus sometimes blend together, in general their focus and typical pattern of expression remain quite distinct. In the one (the Psalms of Thanksgiving) the praise is elicited by God's specific response to need and is stated within the larger context of thanksgiving. In the other (the Hymn of Praise) the praise stems from reflection on who God is, not specifically on what He has just done.

Ten

Psalm 65: Responding to Our Riches

(A Song of Communal Thanksgiving)

In their book *The Search for America's Faith* George Gallup (of Gallup Poll fame) and David Poling chronicle the religious sensibility of contemporary America. Surprising to many, perhaps, is the fact that in 1978 eighty percent of all Americans said they believed Jesus Christ was "God" or the "Son of God." (This is an almost identical percentage to that of 1951.) Eighty-nine percent of the representative poll said similarly that they prayed. And yet fifty-three percent (down from seventy-five percent in 1952) believed religion to be "very important" in their lives.

Gallup discovered in another 1978 poll that while most Americans might believe Jesus is "God," sixty-one million adults were not members of any church or religious group. This was forty-one percent of the adult population. Forty-nine percent of these unchurched Americans (and thirty-nine percent of those attending church!) agreed with the statement that "most churches and synagogues today are *not* effective in helping people find meaning to life." Similarly, eighty-eight percent of the unchurched (and seventy percent of the churched!) agreed that a person could be a good Christian even if he or she did not attend church.

With these and other similar findings, Gallup and Poling paint a picture of contemporary religious life in America. It is a description of widespread but increasingly individualistic and shallow belief. America's "faith" is simultaneously becoming divorced from her life and moving outside the walls of the church. In an in-depth survey made in 1976 of young adults in the Greater Dayton, Ohio area, for example, only twenty-six percent either attended church regularly or responded that religion affected their daily lives "a great deal."

How different this picture of America's faith is from that of the writer of Psalm 65. For the psalmist, to be able to praise God in corporate worship is a great blessing. He expresses his satisfaction with being able to gather with his fellow believers at the Temple. His faith is neither an individualistic nor a "Sunday" affair. Instead, all of life finds its meaning in relation to God the Redeemer, Creator, and Provider. Moreover, the psalmist desires to sing of the fact with his brothers and sisters in the faith. To the question, Could one still be a good believer without collective worship? the psalmist would have responded negatively. The Israelites' faith was corporate; they were the people of God.

Psalm 65: A Psalm of Communal Thanksgiving

Psalm 65 is a song of collective thanksgiving to God. Divided into three parts (vv. 1-4; 5-8; 9-13), the hymn does not, until the final stanza, reveal the specific reason for its composition. The poet writes:

Thou visitest the earth and waterest it,
    thou greatly enrichest it;
the river of God is full of water;
    thou providest their grain,
    for so thou hast prepared it.
Thou waterest its furrows abundantly,
    settling its ridges,
softening it with showers,
    and blessing its growth.
Thou crownest the year with thy bounty;
    the tracks of thy chariot drip with
    fatness (vv. 9-11).

The psalm is a hymn of thanksgiving for a plentiful harvest.

Recognizing his dependence on God for all of life, the psalmist, along with his fellow believers, had vowed to God that he would come to the Temple to thank God for His goodness and grace once the harvest was done (v. 1). Perhaps the psalmist's vow was part of the promises made by the Israelite farmers at the time of planting. If so, the setting for this hymn might be a public festival commemorating a successful agricultural year. Some scholars suggest that Israel annually held such a festival of thanksgiving at the end of the rainy season when all Israel came to Jerusalem to fulfill their vows of praise to God (see Lev. 23:33-36). Rather than rest content with their labors, these early Jews recognized that their prosperity was from God.

Others who have studied this psalm suggest that the composer's vow was part of a national lament voiced when drought or crop failure seemed imminent (see chap. 4). Verse 3 might suggest that the psalmist had associated the delay of the rains with

God's punishment for sin, and the abundant showers with His forgiveness. If this is the case, the mention of vows recalls Solomon's prayer at the dedication of the Temple when he petitioned: "When heaven is shut up and there is no rain because they have sinned against thee, if they pray toward this place, and acknowledge thy name, and turn from their sin, when thou dost afflict them, then hear thou in heaven, and forgive the sin of thy servants, thy people Israel, when thou dost teach them the good way in which they should walk; and grant rain upon thy land, which thou hast given to thy people as an inheritance" (1 Kings 8:35,36).

The context of the original law which triggered this response of thanksgiving is uncertain. But in either case (an annual vow related to planting the crops or a vow triggered by the threat of drought), the purpose of the psalm itself is clear: a grateful response to God by His people for a rich harvest. The psalmist is thankful for what his Lord has provided.

Thinking back to the results of the Gallup survey we can observe how different this sense of corporate thanksgiving is than that typical of most Americans. While we may still believe in God and even turn to Him in time of crisis, we for the most part ignore Him in our daily lives when everything is going well. Do we thank Him publicly for a promotion in our employment or a good sale of our cattle? More often we simply feel content over a job well done. When things go well, when life's "riches" come our way, we too often dwell either on these "riches" or on our sense of accomplishment. The sense of dependence on our God which is so real in our time of crisis has disappeared, even for many who truly love Jesus Christ and want to serve Him. Psalm 65 challenges such individualistic and secular thinking. It would have us join with the people of God in praise of His goodness.

Thanksgiving or Praise?

Psalm 65 has caused much debate among scholars, for it has seemed to some to be more a general Hymn of Praise than a specific Psalm of Thanksgiving. Roland Murphy says, for example: "God is praised, not thanked." It is true that the psalm's focus is on God alone. Also, the psalmist uses the more general term for God, *Elohim*, rather than God's revealed name, *Yahweh* (Jehovah), a name more typical of Psalms of Thanksgiving. Moreover, in our discussion of Hymns of Praise (chaps. 7 and 8) we noticed how such psalms focus on God's goodness and greatness, as this one does. Thus it is easy to see why some think Psalm 65 is a Hymn of Praise. But what can be said in answer to such observations is that while the psalm's focus is that of praise, its context (thanksgiving for a rich harvest) is evident from verses 9 and following. *The psalmist chooses to respond to his bounty by giving thanks in the form of praise to God.*

It is God's activity toward His children that is emphasized rather than His being, in and of itself (as is typical of the Hymn of Praise). However, the psalmist's praise focuses on *God's* activity for us, not on our involvement with Him. Rather than risk magnifying the importance of his effort or that of his coworkers, the psalmist limits reference to himself to his recollection of his prayers and his sin (vv. 2,3). As with the composers of psalms of praise, the writer focuses on God alone.

In church recently I heard a minister thank God

for the successful surgery performed on a parishio-
ner that week. He prayed, "Thank you, Lord, for giving the doctors the skill to complete the operation."
The prayer was certainly a valid one, for God does
work through people to accomplish His purposes.
But Psalm 65 offers an alternate format of thanksgiving, one particularly suited to our present egotistical
age. In order to be sure that the focus of our prayer is
upon God and what *He* has done, we might well join
the psalmist in voicing thanksgiving in such a way
that it is indistinguishable from our praise. Rather
than pray, "Thank you, Lord, for giving us the wisdom and skill to know how to plant and fertilize and
cultivate," we might better simply celebrate God's
generosity to us. It is His river, after all, that runs full
of water and His grain that is provided (v. 9). In this
thanksgiving the psalmist is careful that his praise
remains Other-directed. Psalm 65 would have us
focus on the objective side of our faith, on God Himself and His salvation.

Within the context of the successful completion of
the harvest season, the hymn writer is able to envis-
age the fullness of God. A simple "thanks" is not
enough. A perfunctory recognition of God's sovereignty and providence is not sufficient. The bounty of
his crop leads the psalmist to praise God in the wid-
est possible terms. Thus, verses 1 through 4 serve as
an introduction to the psalm, concentrating on God's
grace as Redeemer. The next section, verses 5
through 8, presents God in both His majesty and His
love. God's salvation is again mentioned (v. 5) but the
focus is principally upon God's *greatness* as Creator.
Having proclaimed God's graciousness and greatness
as a foundation for his praise, the psalmist speaks in
the closing stanza concerning the specific occasion

for the hymn—the renewed fertility of the land. He
sees in this a demonstration of God's *goodness* as
Sustainer. The psalm ends on a high note of praise as
even the meadows and valleys shout for joy because of
God's provision.

God Our Redeemer (vv. 1-4). As the psalm opens,
the songwriter asserts what he has learned: praise is
due to the God of Zion. With apprehension he has
sown his seeds and promised to offer sacrifices and
thanksgiving to God if the crop is successful. (Perhaps a drought has heightened his concern.) Now he
is coming to Yahweh's Temple to perform his vow, for
God has heard his prayer. Reflecting upon his gracious God, the psalmist is reminded of his own sin-
fulness. But rather than arousing fear of possible
judgment, his recollection stimulates praise, for he
knows that God has forgiven him. Since for the Israelite sin was typically identified with disaster (the
book of Job discusses exceptions to this general
rule), God's blessing on the harvest is a sure sign to
the poet that his transgressions have been forgiven.
The psalmist has experienced God's presence in the
harvest. Thus, the writer comes to the Temple joy-
fully and expectantly, for he believes that God is calling him to worship.

The motivating reason for the psalmist's praise,
the bounty of the land, is not yet mentioned. The
broader context of God's holiness and grace must
first be proclaimed. One hears in the opening of the
psalm a song to Israel's gracious God—a God who
hears, forgives and draws His people near:

"Blessed is he whom thou dost choose
     and bring near,
          to dwell in thy courts!
We shall be satisfied with the good-

ness of thy house,
thy holy temple!" (v. 4).

As with the writer, our worship should flow out of
our experiences and our work. We should sense God's
guidance and provision in our daily lives and hear in
them His call to come to His house to worship. God's
signature is on all of life. His presence in our daily
tasks should inform and deepen our worship. Life is
interconnected. Yet too seldom do we come to church
expectant and appreciative because of God's leading
during the week. The psalmist is able to see God's
saving grace reflected in one of life's events. For him
the specific leads to the general, the spring showers
recall God's atonement for sin and inspire him to
offer heartfelt worship in God's Temple.

God the Creator (vv. 5-8). To praise God for His
salvation and grace is not sufficient, however. God's
greatness must also be affirmed. In what one writer
has called "the essence of the whole Old Testament
faith," the psalmist expresses in verse 5 his trust in a
God who inspires both love and awe. His God is a God
of salvation who performs great and wondrous deeds.
In portraying this God, the writer celebrates His
power over creation. God is not simply one who calls
us to come into His presence with singing, He is also
the one who has conquered the unruly and chaotic,
putting it in its place. He has established the mountains and quieted the tumult of the people. He has
stilled the menacing sea. Both sun and moon (the
"outgoings" of morning and evening) are in His control, so that all creation shouts for joy.

W. H. Auden has said, "The most commonplace
things are tinged with glory." This is true. It is, however, not the ordinary but the extraordinary which

momentarily captures this psalmist's attention. In the face of God's mighty creative acts, even "those who dwell at earth's farthest bounds are afraid at thy signs" (v. 8). The exact group this phrase is referring to is uncertain. The wording occurs only here in the Old Testament. Either "all the ends of the earth" (see Ps. 67:7) or perhaps the demonic powers God has defeated are in the writer's mind. In either case, his message is clear: God's power over creation is awesome to behold.

In his children's story *The Lion, The Witch, and The Wardrobe* C. S. Lewis casts the Christ-story in the land of Narnia, where Aslan, the Lion, is portrayed as a Christ-figure. The story relates how four children magically find their way into Narnia and learn of the imminent return of Aslan. Fearful that a lion will harm them, the children ask Mr. and Mrs. Beaver, "Is he safe?" To which Mr. Beaver responds, "Of course he's not safe. But he's good." Throughout all his children's stories Lewis returns to this theme over and over: the children can't decide whether being with Aslan is "more like playing with a thunderstorm or playing with a kitten." Though Aslan might allow children to play with his mane, and though he has come back to rescue Narnia from the curse of winter under the White Witch's reign, he is also not beyond scratching them when necessary. And there is never a question as to who is in control of all of Narnia. Lewis's allegory concerning Christ Himself also captures something of the psalmist's perspective of God. God is *good*. He is gracious and forgiving, desiring us to draw near. Yet He is also *God*, the great and awesome God of the universe. Certainly He is not to be domesticated by anyone. He is not tame, although He is gracious.

God the Sustainer (vv. 9-13). Having focused both upon God's immanence and His eminence—that is, having praised Him both for His intimate and gracious regard for His people and His majestic power over all, the psalmist turns his praise, in conclusion, toward the immediate cause for thanksgiving, the rich harvest he has experienced. It is this which has inspired his reflection upon God's creative acts in history and His forgiveness of the sins of humankind. Now, with perhaps a voice anticipating future harvests as well, the psalmist vividly offers praise for the blessings of the past year. Painting a succession of colorful landscapes, he sets forth his delight in spring and summer. There is not a single word about men and women, their labor or their abilities. Rather, God alone is celebrated. It is *His* tracks which "drip with fatness," that is, with goodness. The word picture is perhaps of God's chariot riding throughout the heavens showering abundance on all (see Ezekiel's vision of God riding a throne chariot, Ezek. 1:15-28). Or perhaps the picture is of an overflowing farmcart dropping some of its contents. In either case, the meaning is similar: God richly provides.

The full extent of God's provision for His creation becomes clear as the psalmist concludes his hymn. The wilderness which ordinarily would be barren and drab has become a green pasture. So too the hills which are personified as living creatures who "gird themselves with joy." The flocks grazing in the field seem like flowing robes adorning the meadow, and similarly the valleys are covered with grain. The psalmist's joy in living in God's world is apparent. Awakened to God's grace and greatness, the writer hears from God the music of life's goodness. It is not merely the poet who is shouting and singing for joy. All of creation has joined the chorus. Truly life in the presence of God is glorious.

Conclusion

The recognition that God should be worshiped, for He is responsible for the "common" blessings of life which we experience, is not limited to the Old Testament. Paul, in at least three instances, argues that God is to be worshiped by all peoples because His gracious provision for humankind is evident to all who will hear. In Lystra, for example, after Paul and Barnabas heal a crippled man, the townspeople mistake them for gods. But the apostles respond: "We also are men, of like nature with you, and bring you good news, that you should turn from these vain things to a living God who made the heaven and the earth and the sea and all that is in them. In past generations he allowed all the nations to walk in their own ways; yet he did not leave himself without witness, for he did good and gave you from heaven rains and fruitful seasons, satisfying your hearts with food and gladness" (Acts 14:15-17). The people of Lystra should have known something of the living God through His activity as Creator and Provider. It is this "general revelation" that Paul attempts to build on as he presents the gospel.

A similar strategy is used by Paul in Athens. There he argues for the truth of the gospel based in the Athenians' worship of an unknown God: "The God who made the world and everything in it, being Lord of heaven and earth . . . is [not] served by human hands, as though he needed anything, since he himself gives to all men life and breath and everything. And he made from one every nation of men . . . that they should seek God, in the hope that they might feel after him and find him. Yet he is not far from each one of us, for 'In him we live and move and have our being' " (Acts 17:24-28). Again, Paul bases his argument on general revelation, on the fact that even the Athenians seek after God who provides "life and breath and everything."

A third example is given in Paul's letter of introduction to the Romans. In setting out his theology for a church he hopes soon to visit, Paul begins his explanation of the gospel by describing God's wrath against men and women because they suppress the truth: "For what can be known about God is plain to them, because God has shown it to them. Ever since the creation of the world his invisible nature, namely, his eternal power and deity, has been clearly perceived in the things that have been made. So they are without excuse" (Rom. 1:19,20).

Paul's argument is that all humankind should be honoring God and giving thanks to Him for God has revealed Himself in all His activity on our behalf (see v. 21). Yet we have senselessly turned away from such knowledge and become fools.

In each instance Paul recognizes, as does our psalmist, that the glory of a successful harvest is meant to turn us to God in worship. Our experience of God the Creator and Sustainer should open our minds and hearts to receive the good news of God the Redeemer.

God's goodness causes the psalmist to praise God's grace in forgiving his sins. For most of the Athenians and for those Paul describes in Romans 1, such general revelation has no such effect. Instead they become fools, rejecting the glory of the immortal God. Life, all life, is a witness to God's glory, goodness, and grace. Even our accomplishment, our work, is not fundamentally *our* achievement, but God's, who showers blessings upon us all. Psalm 65 is a reminder to us to look for God in all we do. It is also a call for us to thank God for all He has done.

Discussion Questions

1. Why do you think the psalmist does not begin his hymn by mentioning his successful harvest?

2. How is God portrayed in this psalm? What chief qualities does He have?

3. Psalm 79:13 records a vow by God's people to praise Him after God rescues them from danger. How might this verse help us understand verse 1 of our psalm?

4. Where does the psalmist find God's signature on life? Where have you experienced the presence of God?

5. Psalm 65:9-13 is a particularly good example of Old Testament poetry (see chap. 1). Can you find both synonymous and synthetic parallelism? What images are used? Is there poetic hyperbole (exaggeration)?

6. Why don't more people turn to God when they are blessed? Romans 1:19-23 offers an answer.

7. How central is public praise in your life? What is your response when you are blessed by God?

Eleven

Psalm 72: The King and the KING

(A Royal Psalm)

Do you recall where you were when John F. Kennedy was assassinated? I was on top of a sixty-foot pile of scrapwood, preparing a bonfire for the pep-rally before the Stanford-University of California football game. Once the news became clear we climbed down and went back to our dormitories. There would be no bonfire or football game that week. "Camelot" had ended. It did not really matter what our political affiliation. What had happened to our president had in a real sense affected us all.

Such close identification with our leaders is by no means unique. It is repeated in all lands at all times. When Prince Charles announced his engagement to Lady Diana, there was celebration throughout England and women even cut their hair in a new style modeled after that of the future queen. We look to our leaders for inspiration and example. We also pray for our leaders that they will promote peace and justice and that through them there will be abundance and blessing for all. Although we may have a nagging suspicion that our political leaders might not be equal to our hopes, we still place our confidence in them, and our hopes and fears rise and fall with their fortunes.

Certainly the presidency of Ronald Reagan has been but one more example of this.

In like manner, Israel centered its aspirations in its king. In the book of Psalms we have a number of prayers sung on behalf of the kings. These Royal Psalms (for example, Pss. 2; 18; 21; 45; 72; 110) were sung to and for the king at his coronation and at his marriage, during his preparations for battle and at his victory celebrations. Throughout the ancient Near East, such prayers for royalty were commonly uttered. Usually the language was flattering and extravagant. Ancient peoples, like men and women today, wanted the best for their leaders.

But in Israel's case there was also something unique about their prayers for their king, unique because their prayers were rooted in *past* promises by their God. In the Psalms we do not hear merely the common Oriental hyperbole associated with good wishes for royalty. Rather, prayers are offered for the Davidic ruler based on the promise to David by our Lord that He would establish His throne with David forever (see 2 Sam. 7; Ps. 132). God's covenant was His pledge to work through David and his descendents. Because God had joined with His people through their king, because He had chosen to be their God in this way, Israelite songwriters freely asked on behalf of their king for justice and peace, long life and rich harvests, world dominion and blessing.

The psalmist's model for his prayers, at times, was Solomon. If only the present king could live up to Solomon's ideal, if only he could create a responsible and effective government as Solomon had, then all would be well. Psalm 72 is one such psalm. It is a psalm dedicated to Solomon and his glory. (The title

"A Psalm of Solomon" can mean in the Hebrew "concerning Solomon," or "in honor of Solomon," as well as "by Solomon.") Psalm 72 sings the praise of Solomon's reign in order to portray the present blessing desired for the psalmist's king (see vv. 8, 10, 15). The past is used as a paradigm, a model that the author prays God will duplicate.

At the same time, Psalm 72 points in another direction as well. For even Solomon was not an ideal king. Solomon not only had the Queen of Sheba come bearing gifts, he also instituted forced labor (1 Kings 9) and created a "heavy yoke" for his people (1 Kings 12). And what was true of Solomon proved true of his successors. Neither past nor present kings could fulfill Israel's dreams. Thus, this psalm, like others of Israel's Royal Psalms, came to be understood as having a *future* reference, a Messianic hope. Such hope was only heightened when Israel's monarchy came to an end.

The king who was described was more than even Solomon. He was truly a King of Kings, a King Israel had yet to know in the psalmist's day but a King who would one day come. It is this Messianic focus that became the psalm's primary meaning as it was prayed through the centuries and sung in the context of Israel's worship. Israel placed its hope, not only in its king, but in the King of Kings.

Psalm 72 thus provides us both a model for political leadership (a description of what an ideal king would be like) and a picture of the Messiah (a description of the King of Kings). It is both a prayer for God's blessing on the king and a prophecy concerning the Christ who was to come. Although the original songwriter's focus was no doubt on his king, his inspired words had a fuller meaning than he could know, a meaning that future Jews and Christians have recognized.

Concerning the King

The model which Psalm 72 provides of a political ruler is a radically different view than those of the monarchies surrounding Israel. Most ancient peoples (as is true also of most modern peoples) thought of *power* as the basis of authority. (They believed that "might makes right.") The writer of Psalm 72, however, pictures a ruler who is (1) dependent on God alone and (2) able to bring about continuing prosperity and establish worldwide dominion only because of his righteous and just dealings, particularly with respect to the poor.

It is important to note the original context of the psalm. It was more than likely first sung at the coronation of a king of Israel, or perhaps at one of the anniversary celebrations of the king. But though the psalm is a prayer in honor of the king, its fundamental perspective is that God alone is "King." He is the one responsible for the peace and prosperity (the *shālōm*, v. 3) of both ruler and people. The psalm begins and ends with the realization that God alone is the source of righteousness and its consequent blessings:

Give the king thy justice, O God,
  and thy righteousness to the royal son!
(v. 1)
Blessed be the Lord, the God of Israel,
  who alone does wondrous things.
Blessed be his glorious name for ever;
  may his glory fill the whole earth!
  Amen and Amen! (vv. 18,19).

For the Jews, God was their true King, and the temporal king had only derivative power. Even David had to be reminded of this fact by Nathan the prophet (2 Sam. 12). The psalmist reinforces this perspective concerning his king by using the word "thy" four times in the opening two verses in reference to God. It is "thy" justice ("thy righteousness") which is needed on behalf of "thy" people ("thy poor"). In the context of his coronation, the king is to be humbled with the reminder that even he is dependent on God.

The psalmist's prayer for his king is in one sense threefold: that his God-given righteousness and justice (1) would bring about national prosperity (vv. 1-7), (2) would create international dominion (vv. 8-14), and (3) would prove long lasting (vv. 15-17). But there is, at a more basic level, one overarching request which dominates the psalm: the desire for the king to be given the ability to rule justly. The national blessings spelled out in verses 2 through 7 are dependent on the gift of divine justice requested in verse 1. Similarly, the worldwide dominion asked for in verses 8 through 11 hinges on the viewpoint that the king "delivers the needy" and "the poor and him who has no helper" (vv. 12-14). The request for longevity for the king in verses 15 through 17 seems best understood as the means of ensuring a continuing just reign.

But what is this "justice" that is sought? How is it to be defined? Our society usually gives one of two answers to this question. "Justice" means either "to each his due" (that is, according to merit) or "to each one equally" (that is, "one person, one vote"). Listen, however, to the description of God's justice as given in Psalm 72:

May he judge thy people with righteousness,
> and thy poor with justice!
Let the mountains bear prosperity [*shālōm*]
> for the people,
> and the hills, in righteousness!
May he defend the cause of the poor of
> the people,
> > give deliverance to the needy,
> > and crush the oppressor! (vv. 2-4).

Rather than any evenhanded or meritorious
standard of justice, the psalmist seems here to
equate justice with acting on the side of the poor and
needy. The king is to exercise his righteousness by
giving to each according to his or her need. Prosperity for the people is linked with the cause of the poor
of the people (v. 4). Similarly, the psalmist links the
king's international reputation not with the fact that
he is rich or powerful, but that he has pity on the
weak and finds their blood precious (vv. 13,14). The
psalmist asks that the king become famous *because*
("for," v. 12) "he delivers the needy when he calls."
Here is the writer's understanding of "justice"!

How strange such a definition of justice is to most
of us. "Compassion," yes. "Benevolence," sure. But is
this justice? Jeremiah offers a confirming viewpoint
for this biblical understanding of justice as he
announces God's judgment on King Jehoiakim
because of his injustice. He prophesies:

> Woe to him who builds his house by un-
> righteousness,
> > and his upper rooms by injustice;
> who makes his neighbor serve him for
> nothing,

and does not give him his wages;. . .
Did not your father eat and drink
and do justice and righteousness?
Then it was well with him.
He judged the cause of the poor and
needy;
then it was well.
Is not this to know me?
says the Lord (Jer. 22:13-16).

Certainly the biblical view of justice includes aspects of equality and merit. We are to pay appropriate wages and treat our neighbor fairly, as Jeremiah recognizes. But there is also a conspicuous and dominating concern for the poor and needy. It is this seeking of justice for those who are suffering which is even viewed as one evidence of "knowing God."

The God of Psalm 72 has a special concern for the poor. The poor are not idealized; oppression and violence are their fare (v. 14). Neither is God's activity limited to them; His righteousness as mediated through the king is to be "like rain that falls on the mown grass, like showers that water the earth!" (v. 6). Moreover, it will attract kings from "Tarshish" and "the isles" (the remote west), as well as from "Sheba" and "Seba" to the south (v. 10). Nevertheless, the king, as God's spokesperson, is portrayed as particularly involved with those without a helper (v. 12)! Like the Exodus event when God acted to fulfill His promises to His people by taking sides with the oppressed, and like the prophets' message which proclaimed that God would destroy Israel not only because of her idolatry but also because of her mistreatment of the poor, so Psalm 72 reveals that God is concerned with delivering the weak and needy.

Politics, like religion, is something we are sometimes told not to discuss publicly for fear of offending people. Even in the church, where religion is freely discussed, politics is often an unspoken issue. But Psalm 72 is a political psalm and requires of us a political response. In the prayer for Israel's king we hear the question, Have we allowed the values of our affluent society to shape our thinking and acting toward the poor? Is our country's international recognition based on our attitude toward the needy? Does our government actively side with those who have no helper? And should we? Do we seek to crush the oppressor, *all* oppressors? Do we citizens vote for those who show a particular concern for the poor? These are explosive questions, but ones which Psalm 72 itself suggests. Such questions *need to be asked* probingly by those in both major political parties. The psalmist is neither Republican nor Democrat, but neither is he politically indifferent. His prayer challenges us, asking, Are we willing to argue for a concept of justice that begins from the side of the poor?

The stakes, as the psalmist presents them, are high. This prayer for the king to have a divinely-based justice which watches out for the needy carried with it large expectations. Because earthly blessings were viewed as a sign of God's favor in response to their keeping His Law (see Deut. 30:15-20), the psalmist expected that peace and prosperity would follow from the administration of justice for as long as the "sun endures" (v. 5). If the king ruled as God would, there would even be harmony between humankind and nature once again. It is this hope for a king who will act justly that causes the psalmist to request that there be grain in the land, even on the tops of the mountains where the least fertile soil usually is found (v. 16). If the king will rule justly, the psalmist is confident that "peace [will] abound, till the moon be no more" (v. 7). Moreover, he is confident that all kings will "fall down before him, all nations serve him" (v. 11). Under such a king, both people and produce will "blossom" (v. 16). Surely "his name [will] endure for ever" (v. 17).

The King of Kings

Such a portrayal of a righteous king—a perfect ruler—had, as we have observed, an ideal quality to it which none of Israel's kings possessed, not even Solomon. Recall how his son, Rehoboam, summarized Solomon's rule: "My father chastised you with whips, but I will chastise you with scorpions" (1 Kings 12:11). In the end, Solomon's rule lacked justice toward the poor. And partly for this reason, his empire was fleeting. At his death, in fact, his kingdom splintered. There was no lasting peace and prosperity. Similarly, his worldwide influence proved ephemeral. And what was true of Solomon was true in greater or lesser degrees of all of Israel's kings. And it is true of all kings and rulers. "Power corrupts and absolute power corrupts absolutely." The truth of this proverb has been demonstrated repeatedly.

Psalm 72 was, thus, a prayer whose expectations were frustrated. It did not seem to be answered in Israel's lifetime, as few kings proved just or their peaceful reigns long lasting or widely influential. When the monarchy was destroyed in 587 B.C. by Babylonia, one would have expected Psalm 72 to be neglected and eventually forgotten. For then there wasn't even a king in Israel with any power. But Psalm 72 was handed down and preserved, for God

promised to rule through the line of David forever.
The psalm came to be understood as a prophecy of
the coming Messiah, the future Son of David, the
true King of Kings. And in the early church, also, the
psalm was recognized as a description of Jesus Himself. Jesus was the Christ, the Messiah, the Son of
David, the King, the Ruler. He was the embodiment
of all of Israel's hopes and dreams for her ruler—and
all our hopes and dreams.

For Jesus was *just*. As the Messiah, Jesus
embodied the psalmist's notion of "to each according
to his or her need." When He inaugurated His teaching ministry, for example, Jesus opened the book of
the prophet Isaiah in the synagogue and read:

> The Spirit of the Lord is upon me,
> because he has anointed me to preach
>   good news to the poor.
> He has sent me to proclaim release
>   to the captives
> and recovering of sight to the blind,
> to set at liberty those who are
>   oppressed,
> to proclaim the acceptable year of
>   the Lord (Luke 4:18,19).

And then Jesus said to all who were present, "Today
this Scripture has been fulfilled in your hearing" (v.
21). Jesus' mission as King of Kings was to all, but
particularly to the poor and blind and oppressed. He
healed them. He ate in their houses. He died for
them. Such an orientation toward the weak by a ruler
is thought foolishness by some. But for those needing such "justice," it is truly redemptive; it was certainly to the woman taken in adultery and to the man
who couldn't walk. Jesus' justice was and is partial to
the needy.

Martin Luther struggled to earn Jesus' favor. He sought a disciplined, righteous life. But the thought of God's judgment paralyzed him with fear, for who really could be thought worthy in God's eyes? Do any of us want to be judged by God according to our merit? Or even by a divine standard applied equally to all? Martin Luther found no inner peace as he envisioned himself before God, his just ruler, until he read Romans 1:16,17: "For I am not ashamed of the gospel: it is the power of God for salvation to everyone who has faith. . . . For in it the righteousness of God is revealed through faith for faith." What Luther discovered was an understanding of God's righteousness, His justice that echoes Psalm 72.

God's righteousness as embodied in Jesus Christ is not a threat. Rather it has to do with delivering the needy who call and the poor who have no helper (Ps. 72:12). It is the substance of the gospel, the good news that in Jesus Christ, God the judge is also the one who assumed the penalty, dying on the cross for helpless sinners.

Not only is Jesus just, as King of Kings His reign of *peace and prosperity* is to be *forever*. Psalm 72 recognized that the perfect king would live "while the sun endures" and his peace would abound "till the moon be no more" (vv. 5,7). A just king who briefly rules and brings only the beginning of peace and prosperity accomplishes little. But the resurrection of the King of Kings confirms the continuing vitality of His reign. Jesus Christ's ongoing life demonstrates and ensures the efficacy of His death on the cross for us. His unique sense of justice on behalf of needy sinners will endure. Paul writes, "If Christ has not been raised, your faith is futile and you are still in your sins" (1 Cor. 15:17). It is God's justice that we need. It is His gracious, righteous activity on behalf of the outcast that is crucial. But without duration, without the continued flourishing of His peace "till the moon be no more" (Ps. 72:7), our confidence would be in vain.

The picture of the King of Kings in Psalm 72 is, first, of someone who delivers the needy. It is the image of a just king which found its fulfillment in the cross. It is an image which was foolish to the Greek but which is the power of salvation to all who believe. Second, Psalm 72 portrays a King of Kings whose peace continues while the sun endures. Here is an image that found its confirmation in the empty tomb. It is the power of the cross that Christians preach, but this is based in the reassuring and ongoing light of the Resurrection. Third, Psalm 72 presents the King of Kings as one who will have *worldwide dominion*. The picture is of friend and foe bowing before him:

> May he have dominion from sea to sea,
>   and from the River to the ends of
>   the earth!
> May his foes bow down before him,
>   and his enemies lick the dust!
> May the kings of Tarshish and of the isles
>   render him tribute,
> May the kings of Sheba and Seba bring
>   gifts!
> May all the kings fall down before him,
>   all nations serve him! (vv. 8-11)

Has this happened? Not yet, but we look forward to its reality at Christ's second coming. Although the King of Kings inaugurated His reign, although the divine form of justice has been demonstrated and confirmed, the world has yet to pay homage to their ruler. The kingdom has come; yet it needs still to be fully revealed. It is like the leaven which is yet to cause the bread to rise fully (Matt. 13:33). There is a tension that characterizes the Christian life today. Although the good news of Easter is that the cross has ongoing significance, Easter awaits its completion at Christ's reappearing. John, in the book of Revelation, gives us a picture of that final celebration, a picture that complements the prayer of the psalmist. He writes: "Then I looked, and I heard . . . every creature in heaven and on earth and under the earth and in the sea, and all therein, saying, 'To him who sits upon the throne and to the Lamb be blessing and honor and glory and might for ever and ever!' " (Rev. 5:11-13).

Discussion Questions

1. How is "justice" defined by this psalmist?

2. What references to Solomon can be found in the psalm? How are we to understand Solomon's relationship to this psalm?

3. Why does the psalmist want worldwide dominion for the king? Why should other kings render him tribute?

4. The first word of verse 12 can be translated either "for" or "if" or "surely." (This chapter has argued that "for" is preferable.) What difference in meaning would each of these translations make?

5. How should verse 20 be understood (see chap. 1)?

6. Does Psalm 72 provide any help for understanding the role of government today?

7. What comparisons can be drawn between this prayer for Israel's king and Jesus, the Messiah?

Twelve

Psalm 37: Learning Not to Fret

(A Wisdom Psalm)

All of us know people who seem to enjoy life immensely. They have a generally positive outlook toward life that is enviable. Although they are occasionally (or even often) disappointed, they seem able to shrug off life's problems and focus upon its possibilities. This we admire.

As I have been writing this book, I have been living temporarily in Berkeley, California where I am a visiting professor. I have been renting an apartment around the corner from a fruit stand operated by a hardworking, cheerful young owner whom I occasionally see enjoying his lunch with his preschool-aged son. Not knowing me, and without my having any local identification, he cashes my check. He cashes it in Berkeley, California where no one tends to trust another. There is something *right* about this. We sense that here is how life is meant to be lived.

We read with admiration stories of business people who still operate by their word of honor and who trust their associates. In a dog-eat-dog world, some seem able to rise above this, and their happiness and general well-being are apparent to all.

But how difficult it is to adopt such an approach to life. It is so easy to get sidetracked by life's exceptions. My young daughter is preparing for a concert with her classmates and loves it. However, because of an argument with the girl next door with whom she rides to class, she refuses to attend her practice sessions. She lets a momentary wrong interfere with something more important and lasting (even to her, not to mention to her parents). Of course, she is only five and life is still unpredictable.

But what is true of my daughter is true of most of us. We like our jobs, and yet an injustice perpetrated by a fellow worker is allowed to fester to the point that we quit (or are dismissed). We love our spouse, but one act of unfaithfulness is sufficient to turn us in spite against him or her. We involve ourselves in a church program until the local gossip slanders us and we retaliate in kind. Rather than act on what is generally the case, we too often react to what are life's exceptions. Rather than concentrate on the good, we focus on the evil.

It is this situation that the writer of Psalm 37 addresses. Given the fact that wrongdoers sometimes prosper, what should we do? Should we seek to undermine their positions? Should we fight fire with fire? Is it right that we become angry at the injustice of it all? Are we not justified in being bitter about the treatment we sometimes get? The psalmist responds with a simple No. "Fret not yourself because of the wicked," he advises. Instead, continue to "trust in the Lord, and do good" (vv. 1,3).

Some find such advice to be irresponsible exaggeration which does not stand up to life's reality. They consider it on a par with the advice to young suitors to take a cold shower. But surely the basic perspective of Psalm 37 is lost upon such critics. Here is not a naive religious optimism, a banal list of platitudes incapable of actually addressing life situations. Rather, Psalm 37 expresses with calm serenity and confidence—a confidence that is grounded in faith in God and tested through a lifetime of experience—that life from God can be trusted. God has created us such that our existence has certain discernible patterns. We need not be overcome by the way of the wicked. "Better is a little that the righteous has than the abundance of many wicked" (v. 16).

Psalm 37: A Wisdom Psalm

Psalm 37 is one of the Wisdom Psalms, a collection of proverbs that are meant to contrast two basic approaches to existence. Speaking first to his fellow believers and only indirectly to God in prayer, the psalmist has created something of an exception in the Psalter. It is, like the majority of the psalms, a response to God; but the response is mediated through the poet's advice to his listeners. This psalm was used in Israel's worship. However, its primary function was not the praise of God but the instruction of the faithful.

The author is now an old man (v. 25). He addresses his audience much as the wisdom teachers do in Proverbs ("Hear, O sons, a father's instruction," Prov. 4:1; see also Prov. 2:1; 3:1). His intention is *practical*, to persuade his "students" to trust in God despite the presence of the wicked. Any temptation to envy or anger, any pressure from poverty or affliction, any doubt as to God's righteousness or steadfastness, any weariness in the face of adversity must be countered.

Like Psalm 119 or Proverbs 31, the psalm's framework is an *acrostic*, the twenty-two letters of the Hebrew alphabet successively introducing each section (usually a double verse, although the numbering of the verses doesn't exactly correspond). Because of this carefully polished literary structure, the poet feels little need to tie his thought together tightly. There is, instead, merely a common theme—the contrast between the way of the righteous and the way of the wicked.

The reader of Psalm 37 should find himself reminded of the book of Proverbs. There are, in fact, marked similarities between certain verses in Psalm 37 and others found in Proverbs. Thus the psalm's opening verse, "Fret not yourself because of the wicked, be not envious of wrongdoers!" finds its counterpart in Proverbs 24:19, "Fret not yourself because of evildoers, and be not envious of the wicked." Similar comparisons can be made between verse 16 and Proverbs 15:16, between verse 23 and Proverbs 20:24, and between verses 35 and 36 and Proverbs 7:6-9.

As in Proverbs, the psalm uses typical "wisdom" forms of speech. Besides the pattern of an acrostic and the reference to the wisdom of age (v. 25), the psalm employs such common wisdom devices as "better sayings" ("Better is a little . . . than . . ." v. 16; see also Prov. 19:1), first person narrative ("I have seen a wicked man . . ." vv. 35,36; see also Prov. 7:6-9), figurative language ("they . . . fade like the grass," v. 2; see also Prov. 11:22), and admonitions ("Take delight in the Lord . . ." v. 4; see also Prov. 16:3). It is not only in form, however, that Psalm 37 reminds the reader of Proverbs. Its content is similar as well: a life of piety is honored (vv. 3-7), the righteous and the wicked are contrasted (vv. 16,17), God's providence is recognized (vv. 23,24), charity is advised (vv. 25,26), warnings against evil are given (v. 27), and wisdom and justice are closely associated (v. 30).

In all these ways and others, Psalm 37 demonstrates itself to be part of the Wisdom Literature of the Old Testament (also Proverbs, Job, Ecclesiastes). Central to the Wisdom Literature is the recognition that true wisdom is divinely given: "The fear of the Lord is the beginning of wisdom; a good understanding have all those who practice it" (Ps. 111:10). This saying is found in Psalm 111, a hymn of praise to the Lord, but it appears also in Job 28:28 and is repeated several times in the book of Proverbs (1:7; 2:5; 9:10). The pursuit of wisdom is not a secular enterprise. Wisdom is a gift from the Lord with special authority over us (Prov. 2:6). "The teaching of the wise" is a "fountain of life" (Prov. 13:14), and those who ignore it invite death. Here is Psalm 37's perspective. Its reflection on life's two ways is offered in the context of worship. It is done in "fear," that is, in loving and reverent knowledge of the Lord:

> The mouth of the righteous utters wisdom,
>> and his tongue speaks justice.
> The law of his God is in his heart;
>> his steps do not slip (Ps. 37:30,31).

Two Ways of Living

Basic to the Old Testament is the fundamental belief that God blesses the good and punishes the evil. "Seek good, and not evil, that you may live," pleads the prophet Amos (Amos 5:14). As Israel lived its life within the covenant that God made with her, she was taught by the Lord that there are two basic ways of living, each with its attendant consequences. Faithfulness to God and obedience to His Law bring life; compromise and disobedience invite death.

Such an understanding of life's fundamental options was part of the unique revelation of God to Israel, His people. But this realization was not dependent on special revelation alone. God, Israel's Redeemer, was also God the Creator and Provider. And thus life itself reflected this same polarity. "Your sin will find you out" (Num. 32:23) is a common fact of life, as well as a biblical truth. "He who oppresses the poor to increase his own wealth, or gives to the rich, will only come to want" (Prov. 22:16). Such a warning is given in Scripture, but its original source was the observation of how life demonstrates itself to be. And people through the ages have confirmed this basic truth. God has created life in such a way that there are, in fact, two broadly-defined avenues we can travel. The one leads to success; the other, failure. Although the evildoer may seem to be prospering for a time, his profits are temporary. As Proverbs observes, "A wicked man earns deceptive wages, but one who sows righteousness gets a sure reward" (Prov. 11:18).

It is this perspective of the two ways open to humankind, a viewpoint rooted in creation itself, that provides the basic structure of Psalm 37. Two types of individuals are compared and contrasted as to their life-styles and fortunes. The *wicked* plots and gnashes his teeth (Ps. 37:12); he fights against the needy (v. 14); borrows without paying back (v. 21); seeks "to slay" the righteous (v. 32); and is overbearing (v. 35). The *righteous*, on the other hand, is generous and giving (vv. 21, 26); his steps are from the Lord (v. 23); his mouth utters wisdom and speaks justice (v. 30); God's law is in his heart (v. 31); and he is blameless and upright, a person of peace (v. 37).

Each of these two ways, moreover, has its own appropriate reward. The *wicked* will perish, fade like grass (vv. 2, 20); they are laughable to God (v. 13); they will be cut off from their inheritance (vv. 9, 22, 28, 38); after a time they will be no more (vv. 10, 36); their arms will be broken (v. 17); they will perish by their own swords (v. 15); they will be destroyed (vv. 34, 38); they will vanish like smoke (v. 20). The *righteous*, on the other hand, will dwell in the land—that is, will receive their promised inheritance from God (vv. 3, 9, 11, 22, 29, 34); will be given their desires (v. 4); will be vindicated (v. 6); will delight in prosperity (vv. 11, 19); will be upheld by the Lord (v. 17); will abide forever (vv. 18, 27, 28, 29); will be protected by the Lord (vv. 24, 33, 39) and not forsaken (v. 25); salvation is theirs (v. 39); their children will be a blessing (v. 26).

What can we say about the psalmist's bold contrast? We have already suggested two observations: First, his general comments concerning life's two ways are consistent with God's special revelation to His people. This same pattern is found both in the Law and the Prophets. And the psalmist alludes to this fact in the psalm itself. The blessing to the faithful is in the fact that they will "dwell in the land." Here is a clear reference to the promise to Abraham (Gen. 12:1-3). Similarly, the righteous is said to have the law in his heart (Ps. 37:31).

Second, although the two ways are often presented biblically in terms of God's covenant with His people (see Deut. 30:15-20), they are not described in this psalm primarily from that perspective. It is not the covenant that justifies the psalmist's assertions, but life itself. The blessing upon Abraham is not the proof of the matter, but an illustration, an analogy of a general pattern observable in creation. Righteousness is commended for it works; wickedness is condemned for it doesn't. Life is our authority here. It would be wrong to label the psalmist's perspective mere observation. It is not disinterested, scientific judgment at work here, but neither is it a conclusion based on God's special covenant. Instead, the psalmist recognizes that life has certain sacred patterns, created and sustained by God Himself. The godly person, reflecting on creation and on the Creator, will understand the basic options open to all humankind.

Third, this bald stating of the alternatives does not exclude the exception. It merely refuses to dwell upon it. The occasion for the psalm, in fact, is the recognition that the wicked sometimes flourish. ("Be not envious of wrongdoers," v. 1, the psalmist advises). But there is a larger, general pattern that needs to be remembered. Other psalms and wisdom books will deal with the limits of wisdom's two ways (see Ps. 73; Job and Eccles.). It is also a fact that things do not always work out as they should. But the psalmist would have us know that in the course of his years and within the context of his faith in God's righteousness he has observed that virtue *is* rewarded and vice punished. With the writer of Proverbs, he is willing to state the rule and allow for tension, given the exception: "In the path of righteousness is life, but the way of error leads to death" (Prov. 12:28).

But What of Evil?

Psalm 37 is a practical psalm. Its intention is not to deal theoretically with the relationship of God and evil, but to offer advice to God's people as they encounter injustice around them. What should be our response to wickedness that is prospering? Based on the recognition of life's basic options, the psalmist gives a two-fold answer: (1) We are not to fret, but (2) to trust in the Lord and do good.

Fret not yourself (vv. 1, 7, 8); the "doctrine" of the two ways stands. Given the psalmist's faithful observation and reflection on life's overarching pattern, he advises that we need not concern ourselves with what seems the exception. The psalmist counsels that we take the long view of events. We are not to be captured by the tyranny of the immediate. Although "the enemies of the Lord are like the glory of the pastures" (v. 20), this needs to be understood in both its senses. Yes, they are presently glorious. But remember, "they will soon fade . . . and wither" (v. 2). They will vanish—"Like smoke they vanish away" (v. 20). Similarly, although the righteous might fall, "he shall not be cast headlong, for the Lord is the stay of his hand" (v. 24). The psalmist's faith interacting with the experiences of life allows him to assert both the downfall of the wicked and the preservation of those who love God.

God will intervene (vv. 4, 5, 17, 23, 33); have hope. The psalmist emphasizes God's active involvement on behalf of the faithful. The Lord is portrayed as giving those who delight in Him their desires (v. 4). He will act on behalf of those committed to Him (v. 5). "He establishes him in whose way he delights" (v. 23). He will not let the righteous be condemned (v. 33). Those who wait for Him will be exalted "to possess the land" (v. 34). The promises of active intervention on behalf of the faithful are numerous in this psalm:

The salvation of the righteous is from
    the Lord;
    he is their refuge in the time of
    trouble.
The Lord helps them and delivers them;
    he delivers them from the wicked,
    and saves them,
    because they take refuge in him (vv.
    39, 40).

The wicked will perish (vv. 2, 9, 10, 13, 15, 17 and
so on); know this for a certainty. The psalmist portrays the process of destruction for wrongdoers as
inevitable and self-fulfilling. The wicked sow the
seeds of their own destruction. Just as the grass
fades and the green herb withers, know that the
wicked will have his day. The prospect is so certain
that God is portrayed as laughing "at the wicked, for
he sees that his day is coming" (v. 13). Certainly God
is working in and through the whole process: "Those
blessed by the Lord shall possess the land, but those
cursed by him shall be cut off" (v. 22). But it is interesting to note that the emphasis is on judgment as a
"natural" consequence of wrongdoing. Judgment is
God's curse, but it is woven into the very fabric of creation. Those who would carry out evil devices should
know that "whatever a man sows, that he will also
reap" (Gal. 6:7). The psalmist relates what is repeatedly the case:

I have seen a wicked man overbearing,
    and towering like a cedar of Lebanon.
Again I passed by, and, lo, he was
    no more;
    though I sought him, he could not
    be found (vv. 35,36).

Focusing on God and the Good

Psalm 37 responds to the evil person who is prospering by reminding its readers that they need not
fret. There is a God-given pattern of blessings and
curses which align themselves with faithfulness and
faithlessness. Patience is counseled: "Yet a little
while, and the wicked will be no more" (v. 10).

But the psalmist's advice does not end here. It is
not enough to say we should not overly concern ourselves with those who seek our harm. The psalmist
provides as well a counter-perspective: we are to concern ourselves with our Lord. Rather than dwell on
the injustice of life and let our anger build, we need to
redirect our attention toward God. To those who are
tempted and burdened by others who commit wrong,
the psalmist counsels the need to focus on God and
the good.

"Trust in the Lord, and do good" (v. 3). We are not
to respond in kind to those around us, but are
instead to give liberally and lend (v. 26), to speak justice and to utter wisdom (v. 30). Some might say,
"But that is impossible. Such advice would surely
require of one that he or she be almost a saint." And
indeed, this is the case. The psalmist does not counsel that we can turn from evil toward good by the act
of our will alone. Instead he advises us to do so by
first focusing upon God. He does not say, "Do good
and then you will be able to trust God." Rather, he
says, "Trust God—turn your attention toward Him—
and then you will find the resources to rise above the
evil of those around you." If we really believe that
God's judgments are sure, then we are freed from the
need to seek self-vindication.

The psalmist counsels us to "take delight in the

Lord" (v. 4). How easy it is to find our satisfaction in harboring spite toward others. How often we wait for the opportunity to say, "I told you so," or "She is getting what she deserves." But such a preoccupation with the evildoer is frustrating and unsatisfying. If we would have our desires truly fulfilled, if we would find inner contentment, we must truly delight in the Lord. We need not protect our own rights. We need not seek self-justification. It is God who can and will act in our behalf. *"Commit your way to the Lord"* (v. 5). It is His vindication that will satisfy.

The opposite of fretting is being still. To focus on the wrongdoer and his success will only disrupt. But to focus on the Lord allows for a tranquility and calmness. The psalmist's positive advice to those who are agitated by others around them is simply, *"Be still before the Lord, and wait patiently for him"* (v. 7). We are to be meek, not belligerent; the end is certain for both the wicked and the righteous. A self-interested wrongdoing will reap its just desert. But God offers both joy and satisfaction to those who are "his saints" (v. 28).

Conclusion

The advice of Psalm 37 seems almost too simple. Surely we must chafe over and plot against the wrongs done to us. Can we really say, "Don't fret and trust God"? Is it true that the "meek shall possess the land" (v. 11), as the psalm asserts? Such is the question that Jesus' listeners must also have had as they listened to Him echo the words of the psalm: "Blessed are the meek, for they shall inherit the earth" (Matt. 5:5).

Commentators on the Beatitudes have struggled with the proper meaning of the term "meekness." It surely does not mean cowardice or passivity or lack of spirit. Some have found its meaning in the larger cultural use of "meekness" in Jesus' day. For the Greeks, meekness was a primary virtue reflecting the desired mean between excessive anger and the absence of justifiable anger. Aristotle, for example, described as meek the person who is angry on the right occasion with the right people at the right time. But this is not the meaning of the word "meek" in Psalm 37; nor is it the meaning Jesus attached to it. Meekness is not a properly-delegated anger (though this can also be a virtue), but an absence of personal anger and a trusting and submissive attitude toward God. Are we able not to fret? Do we trust in the Lord? Is our delight in Him? Are we committed to letting Him act? Can we be still before Him? Are we willing to continuously do good? If so, we are meek.

Jesus labels such individuals blessed, or happy. They are content. Moreover, it is these who shall inherit the land. Again, Psalm 37 provides the key to understanding the meaning of this promise. Jesus is not promising present wealth, a seaside villa or a stable of horses. He is instead borrowing the imagery of "the promised land." He is emphasizing, as did the psalmist, that God's covenant—His promise to bless His people with land—will hold true. The wicked cannot twist the intention of God's will. What He has arranged—how He has ordered His "estate"—will take place. His promises—His inheritance—will indeed be granted to those who delight in Him.

When greedy, self-serving survivors come to the lawyer of their relative's estate demanding more than their share, my lawyer friends tell me that just the opposite takes place. Rather than work for those whose interest is in themselves, the lawyer would rather work for those whose affection was for the client. Rather than let the wrongdoer, the greedy one, grab the prize, lawyers will often respond in ways that support the "meek." Such is not always the case. But as often as it does take place, it mirrors God's approach to justice. We need not seek to grab the prize. "Better is a little that the righteous has . . . [for] the Lord upholds the righteous" (Ps. 37:16,17).

Discussion Questions

1. What parallels between the book of Proverbs and Psalm 37 can you list?

2. Was this psalm composed in the midst of crisis when all seemed hopeless?

3. Does the fact that Christian children are starving in some parts of the world today call into question verse 25 of the psalm?

4. How is the psalmist's confident assertion of two paths in life, each with its appropriate consequence, meant to function in this psalm? What value does such a belief have?

5. In what way does this psalm express "the power of positive thinking"? In what way is it different?

6. What should be our response to wickedness that is prospering?

For Further Reading

Anderson, A. A. *The Book of Psalms*, vols. 1 and 2. New Century Bible Commentary. Grand Rapids: Eerdmans Publishing Company, 1972.

Anderson, Bernhard. *Out of the Depths: The Psalms Speak for Us Today*. Philadelphia: Westminster Press, 1970.

Bonhoeffer, Dietrich. *Psalms: The Prayer Book of the Bible*. Minneapolis: Augsburg Publishing House, 1970.

Brueggemann, Walter. "From Hurt to Joy, from Death to Life." *Interpretation* 28, January, 1974, pp. 3-19.

Hubbard, David. *Psalms for All Seasons*. Grand Rapids: Eerdmans Publishing Company, 1971.

_____ . *More Psalms for All Seasons*. Grand Rapids: Eerdmans Publishing Company, 1975.

Kidner, Derek. *Psalms*, vols. 1 and 2. Tyndale Old Testament Commentaries. Downers Grove, IL: InterVarsity Press, 1973, 1975.

Lewis, C. S. *Reflections on the Psalms*. New York: Harcrourt, Brace and World, 1958.

Murphy, Roland. *The Psalms, Job*. Proclamation Commentaries. Philadelphia: Fortress Press, 1977.

Terrien, Samuel. *The Psalms and Their Meaning for Today*. Indianapolis: Bobbs-Merrill, 1952.

Weiser, Artur. *The Psalms: A Commentary*. Old Testament Library. Philadelphia: Westminster Press, 1962.

Westermann, Claus. *The Psalms: Structure, Content and Message*. Minneapolis: Augsburg Publishing House, 1980.